LIVRO DA ENSINANÇA DE BEM CAVALGAR TODA SELA

(The Art of Riding on Every Saddle)

Dom Duarte's *Livro da Ensinança de Bem Cavalgar Toda Sela*

"The Art of Riding on Every Saddle"

A Translation into English of King Dom Duarte's 1434 Treatise

Livro Da Ensinança De **Bem Cavalgar** Toda Sela

Written by Duarte, King of Portugal (1391 - 1438)
Translated by
Preto, António Franco (1940 -) and Preto, Luís (1978 -)

ISBN – 13: 978-1461106616
ISBN-10: 1461106613

Cover by Frederico Martins

Information and Disclaimer:

The translation authors do not assume any liability for the use or misuse of any information contained in this book. Practice of any martial arts can be dangerous and guidance of a qualified instructor is advised.

"Men often fail to score a hit ...

... for lack of sight,

poor control of their lances or horses,

or lack of determination."

Duarte, King of Portugal, circa 1434

Acknowledgments

As our readers can surely guess this work is not the result of two men's labour alone. A most qualified and unique team was assembled to make this project possible.

My most sincere thanks are addressed, first of all, to **Dr. Steven Muhlberger.**

His extraordinary knowledge of the medieval period raised hundreds of doubts, questions and suggestions about specific portions of the text. After very open and thorough discussions, appropriate changes were introduced in the first version of my translation, vastly improving the overall quality of the final product (Not to mention his work of elimination of my English shortcomings!).

King Dom Duarte was an enthusiastic and gifted athlete of the art of wrestling; various chroniclers and historians mentioned this fact, namely Ruy de Pina (b.1440 d. 1522), the author of eight-five typed pages about the King's life. He was so fond of this art that he asked his professor of wrestling to describe in some detail its most important techniques, which he included in one chapter of this book. Those three pages were, and still are, totally incomprehensible and impenetrable gibberish to me!

My most sincere thanks to **Mr. Paulo Martins** (Professor of wrestling at one Portuguese university and considered by many our best Olympic wrestler ever) and to **Mr. Greg Mele** (who was able to produce a final version in English of the work done by Mr. Paulo Martins and by **Mr. Luis Preto***). They are the responsible specialists for those pages describing the most important wrestling techniques practiced in Portugal early in the fifteenth century.

My most sincere thanks to Mrs. Kristi Charron for her corrections and suggestions of many terms related to horses and their wild reactions and rebellions against human control.

My most sincere thanks to **Mr. Steve Hick** who was my first contact at the early stages of the project and whose confidence and trust in my ability gave me the required strength to go on with a project that I had considered as "almost impossible" after my first analysis. He was the main responsible for my change of attitude, enabling me to move the project from the "almost impossible" level to a level I can define as "it still looks impossible, but it should be doable!"

The last but not the least, <u>my most sincere thanks also to the co-author of the translation,</u> my son **Mr. Luís Preto** (professor of Physical Education and author of the book *"Jogo do Pau"* – the Portuguese Martial Art of stick fighting).

I finish this note the way I started it, addressing our readers: I hope that when reading Dom Duarte's book you will have at least half the fun we had throughout all the stages of this very special and challenging project!

Antonio Franco Preto   Lisbon,
Spring of 2011

*"*Jogo do Pau*"*: The Ancient Art & Modern Science of Portuguese Stick Fighting,

Author - Luís Preto,

This book was first published by the Chivalry Bookshelf.
(ISBN 1- 891448-31-5)

To the Readers:

António Franco Preto, my father, is an amateur historian and an enthusiastic and persistent researcher.

He saw the translation of Dom Duarte's book as an opportunity to convey to the readers what I consider to be very interesting information related to both his hobbies: History and Researching.

So, he decided to produce two texts to be included in this book; one, before the book 'The Art of Riding on Every Saddle' and the other, just after it.

- A preface to Dom Duarte's book.

He described many events and historical facts that seem at first glance far beyond the expected scope of this work, but he found this to be an unique opportunity to direct the readers attention to some of the events and facts he considered to have been important for the understanding of ourCountry (and for our King Dom Duarte and his book). Not being a professional historian, I am sure he reacted to them in his own way and therefore his choice might be debatable.

All in all, I hope that they, together with Dom Duarte's book, enable the reader to acquire a better understanding of Portugal.

- An article describing the conclusions of his research looking for Dom Duarte's face and forename. Face, because there are no known portraits of him; forename, due to existing discrepancies about it.

I hope you find both of them interesting.
Luís Preto
Spring of 2011

Table of Contents

Preface

Why did we translate King Dom Duarte's book?

I discovered Dom Duarte's book as I researched some historical aspects for my son Luis' book on the Portuguese Art of wooden stick fighting, '*Jogo do Pau*' (published by Chivalry Bookshelf). It was a pleasure to discover that '*Jogo do Pau*"s main striking techniques were exactly the techniques Dom Duarte discusses with the sword; after that, I was very curious about the book, curious enough to spend some considerable time with it. I was absolutely astonished with Dom Duarte's depth of understanding of human behavior and from Dom Duarte's own weaknesses, which serve to humanize him in a unique way. Beyond this, his technical knowledge of the arts of riding, jousting, use of the spear and the sword, and of hunting are unmatched in any historical text with which I am familiar. Enchanted, I spent even more time learning about Dom Duarte's life, and became even more impressed!

Last but not least: I was more than surprised — perhaps even a little disgusted — to find that such an important work, unique in so many aspects, had never been translated into modern Portuguese, much less any other language. That was when, 'The Chivalry Bookshelf' sent an email to my son Luis telling him that the translation into English of Dom Duarte's book was one of the top items on their "wish" list! The stage was set and the stars seemed to align. This is the how and why I took the challenge.

I have to say that it would have been impossible to accept the challenge if I had not been a student of the best (and the toughest) school in Portugal — from age ten to seventeen I was a student of the full-boarded Military School in Lisbon (the *Real Colégio Militar*, called after 1910 simply *Colégio Militar*), where physical activities

[15]

such as riding and fencing were an important aspect of a very demanding educational program (I went from there directly to the University). The grueling program required some fifty hours per week (thirty three of classes and seventeen of studies). Even being a student in the scientific area (Mathematics and Physics were my two major disciplines) I went through seven years of Portuguese (Language and Literature), seven years of History, five years of French, three years of Latin and two years of English; it was a kind of Spartan education (the survival of the fittest, mind and body!).

Portugal became a republic in 1910. If by a touch of magic the monarchy were to return tomorrow, the King of Portugal would be His Royal Highness, *Dom Duarte*, the current and 24th Duke of Bragança.

It is interesting the coincidence of his first name to be *Duarte* and, of specific personal interest to me, the fact that he is also the 28th Earl of Ourém (my place of birth). Also of importance to me is the fact that, in his many public appearances, he always wears in the lapel of his coat the most exclusive pin that identifies him as a former student of "my" *Colégio Militar*.

He is a fine gentleman, taking after his cognomen. When he married in 1995, the government offered him a royal wedding. Many thousands of people watched from the streets and on the official television channel, which carried three full hours of live coverage of the event. Any foreigner would have thought that Portugal was a monarchy and that the King was getting married. I confess I am partial to the guy!

How was the translation done?

Translation is never an easy task. In the case of Dom Duarte's *Livro da Ensinança de Bem Cavalgar toda sela* (known to a handful of those outside of Portugal who know it simply as "Bem Cavalgar"), the task was more difficult than most, for Dom Duarte wrote at the bridge between the fourteenth and fifteenth centuries, and the text has been largely ignored by many scholars who might be expected to have an interest in it; Portuguese and medieval historians, scholars working on the chivalric, combat or equestrian texts, or even by those interested in the corpus of princely handbooks that started to emerge about this time. Dom Duarte's book is all of these—a superb collation of a renowned prince's knowledge from a pivotal period in Portuguese history. But the text is difficult and replete with many instances of unique or nearly unique terms.

The first challenge was finding the text. It survives as but a single medieval manuscript in the French national library (there is but one known original, held now in the *Bibliothèque Nationale de France*, MS Portuguese 5, fol. 99-128). Fortunately, it was copied in 1843 by a copiest of the King's Library in Lisbon, published as *Livro da ensinança de bem cavalgar toda sela, escrito pelo Senhor Dom Duarte, Rei de Portugal e do Algarve e Senhor de Ceuta, transcrito do manuscrito existente na Biblioteca Real de Paris.* (Lisbon: Typ. Rollandiana). More accessible, however, was the 1944 edition by Joseph M. Piel. A comparison of the two showed them to be very similar, saving for some orthographic changes made by Mr. Piel to make the text more accessible. I do not feel these in any way changed the meaning, so Mr. Piel's transcription serves as the foundation for my own translation.

After initial and unsuccessful attempts working straight from the transcribed text—with considerable difficulty—I felt forced to produce the work in two phases. For the first, I wrote in longhand a translation of the whole text into modern Portuguese, because I found that the differences in the syntax between the two languages (a difficulty in many sentences and even for some whole chapters) was too great to enable me to produce an English version directly from the original manuscript.

In the second phase, I translated into English from my version in modern Portuguese. I did this because I wanted to be absolutely sure that I understood— up to the last word—the original manuscript, as my objective was to produce an accurate translation.

The Translation Challenge

While there are different schools of thought on what constitutes an "accurate" translation, my own definition is that it reflects precisely my understanding of what Dom Duarte wanted to convey to the readers of his book. This means not a completely literal translation, but I strove to maintain the exact phrasing as often as possible, but did reserve the right to make minor alterations where necessary to ensure preservation of Duarte's ideas in the English language.

To offer but one example, the translation of the original title for one chapter of Dom Duarte's book: *Dos erros da luyta, brevemente scriptos* (which translates with apparent ease to "The errors of wrestling, briefly written"). Without taking in consideration any evolutionary changes between the modern rules of wrestling and the rules of that fighting art in the fifteenth-century Portugal, I decided to use the word "wrestling" as the translation for *luyta* (the word used by Dom Duarte for the fighting art involving grappling and throws). We do not know whether the wresting in Duarte's experience resembled modern wrestling—be it freestyle, catch-as-catch-can, Greco-Roman, or bits and pieces from every style and from others no longer surviving. Eventually I decided to simply translate it as "wrestling."

[18]

Erros is a word used many times by Dom Duarte throughout his book, always with the same meaning: "errors" or "mistakes." After going through the whole chapter in great detail, I found that in this situation—*and in this situation only*— Dom Duarte used the word not as "errors" but as the "techniques" (which include cunning, stratagems, tricks and deceptions) *that cause the other wrestler to make errors* and through these tactics, to be defeated. Therefore, the final translation of this chapter's title is: *A brief description of wrestling techniques.* The message conveyed is that I had to always challenge my own first translation option, even if it was apparently correct and I felt comfortable with it. The text is full of such landmines, and I hope that I have missed them all.

During the first phase I worked more or less on my own. During the second, I had the invaluable help and support of Dr. Steven Muhlberger, professor of History at Nipissing University, Canada, whose knowledge of medieval history and of the chivalric arts was of the utmost value. Our ongoing dialog produced hundreds of specific challenges to my translation options (not to mention the correction of my many English shortcomings). Lengthy and constructive discussions occurred between us; the most difficult decisions were taken only after we both were in total agreement that we were sure about our understanding of the author's intent.

To augment and reinforce this understanding, it was absolutely essential to spend a great deal of time learning (or in some cases just remembering) about the Portuguese cultural and historical situation and its evolution, about Dom Duarte's way of thinking and his personal life. Given all of this, I do not believe that there were any unsubstantiated assumptions made and that the text will stand as Dom Duarte intended. Or at least I hope it will!

King Dom Duarte and his world

This is going to be, by far, the longest part of my introduction. I apologize in advance to my readers as I am going to describe many events and facts that seem at first glance far beyond the expected scope of this work, but I find this to be an unique opportunity to direct the readers attention to some of the events and facts I consider to have been important for the understanding of my Country (and for our King Dom Duarte and his book). Not being a professional historian, I am sure I have reacted to them in my own way and therefore my choice (and eventually my comments and the writing style) might be debatable.

All in all, I hope that they, together with Dom Duarte's book, enable the reader to acquire a better understanding of Portugal.

In a way I feel somewhat like what I imagine Dom Duarte felt when he decided to have a chapter in his book fully dedicated to wrestling; he wrote he just couldn't resist including it in his book. Some of what follows feels like that.

The Arabs in Portugal and The First Political Crisis

The Arabs

Portugal became, formally, an independent kingdom in 1143, when our first King, Dom Afonso I — known as Dom Afonso Henriques — signed the treaty of Samora (*Zamora*, in the Spanish language) with the King of Leon, formally recognizing the independence of Portugal, with the approval of Cardinal Guido de Vico (the representative of the Pope). The other independent kingdoms in Iberia were, eventually if not all of them simultaneously, Galicia,

Asturias, Navarre, Leon, Aragon, Catalonia, Castile and the Arabic Kingdom with their main cities in Cordoba and Granada.

The Portuguese King Dom Afonso III (1210-1279) conquered the Algarve from the *Arabes* (also called *Mouros*) in 1250, establishing the current Portuguese borders (the Algarve territory was well protected geographically by mountains some thirty miles from the south coast and by a river, *Guadiana*, as its eastern border with Spain). After that conquest, the King of Portugal started to be called, and remained called for many years, the King of Portugal *and* of Algarve. It is interesting to note that it took until 1492 for the Kings of Castile ("Spain") to expel the Arabs from their last Kingdom in the South of Spain (Granada).

Nevertheless, the Arabic communities remained throughout Portugal, duly protected by the Portuguese Kings who needed them for several reasons (even today there is a district in Lisbon called *Mouraria*, where most of the *Mouros* lived). Mixed marriages were common throughout all classes in Iberia during the 11th – 13th centuries. Moorish learning and culture was well advanced; indeed it was more common to know how to write in Arabic than in *Galego*, Portuguese or Castilian). Early in the 14th century the only medical doctors in Portugal were Arabs. Many Arabs (mainly in the Algarve) were landlords of considerable wealth.

It is in this connection that I would first like to introduce King Dom Duarte. It is mentioned that he was forced to directly intervene to fix a local dispute in Elvas, a town at the border with Castile, in 1436 between Christians and Arabs related to the placing of both cemeteries (Arabs from Elvas had very special privileges in recognition of their direct intervention in the war against Castile).

The influence of the Arabic culture remains evident in even our modern language; there are an estimated 700 words in modern Portuguese of Arabic origin (many of them start with *al*). The most common, still used daily by nearly everyone, is *oxalá* (pronounced as "oh-sha-lá"); it means "*Se Deus quiser*" — God willing — and it derives from "Insh'Allah!"

It is in this connection with the Arabs that we can see a glimpse into this great king's progressive human stature. At a time when Christians and Arabs were at war in every respect, material and religious, Dom Duarte — even as a devoted Catholic — financially supported and directly funded many translations into the Portuguese language by Arab poets. How far ahead of his day and how advanced he was relatively to the "politically correct" behavior of 1400. I am sure he got away with it only because he was a Prince and the heir apparent of the Portuguese throne! Unfortunately, the question, "How much was Dom Duarte influenced by Arabic literature?" must remain open; it is a question for a future scholar to examine.

Much more important to me was Dom Duarte's understanding of human behavior and everything behind it, his knowledge of the human weaknesses, some of his "hidden agendas" (which I comment upon in the footnotes), his skills related to introspection, his almost theological comparisons, the linking of horse riding and its related activities to life, his knowledge of the Greek philosophers and of Julius Caesar. His scope was amazing and his depth of knowledge incredible. Can you imagine in the year 1400 how difficult it must have been for one such as he (who read and wrote Portuguese, English, Latin, Greek and some Arabic) to find among his peers someone with whom he could converse, even occasionally if not daily, and exercise his mind, approaching the matters he was really interested in? In fact he mentions this directly in the text, expressing exactly this frustration.

Even by modern standards, his progressive stance towards the Arabs and towards knowledge and human endeavor stands far ahead of his time. You will find many examples of what I have

[22]

described throughout his book, and I hope you enjoy the journey as I did.

The First Political Crisis

King Dom Fernando I died in 1383, (b. 1345) without leaving an heir to the throne of Portugal. This sparked a political crisis and a powerful attempt by the King of Castile to take over the Portugal. It took until April, 1385, for the Portuguese *Cortes* (an embryo of the modern parliament) to elect as King of Portugal and of Algarve, Dom João I, a natural son (born out of wedlock) of the late King Dom Pedro I (b. 1320 – d. 1367), father of King Dom Fernando I.

Following a decisive victory of the Portuguese army — under the direct command of Dom Nuno Álvares Pereira — against Castile, in Aljubarrota (in the center of Portugal), the King of Castile abandoned his claim. In May of 1386, the Portuguese King Dom João I signed an alliance with King Richard II of England. To consolidate it, he married, in February of 1387, Philippa of Lancaster, granddaughter of King Edward III of England, the daughter of the Duke of Lancaster. The crisis was over.

Dom Duarte was their first male son (born in 1391), and the heir apparent to the throne of Portugal.

Only because it is of such importance much later during the second political crisis (1580-1640), I note here that Dom João I had another son (Dom Afonso) born *before* his marriage to Philippa of Lancaster, who he protected throughout all his life. Ultimately, he made him the first Duke of Bragança (a Portuguese town in the North East) and married him, in 1401, to the daughter of his army commander.

[23]

Kings Dom João I and Dom Duarte

King Dom João I (b. 1357 - d. 1433)

Perhaps the most important fact of João's reign to be the already mentioned alliance he established with King Richard II of England and his marriage to Philippa of Lancaster; it not only protected Portugal from Castile (Spain), but because Philippa also became a great Portuguese Queen. One of her important decisions, as far as the education of his son Dom Duarte was concerned, was to send him to stay for a long period in the English Court when he had come of age (when he was at fourteen years old).

In 1411, King Dom João I called his son (then but twenty years of age) to his side and started a permanent training program, progressively sharing and transferring to him the powers of the Crown, enabling Dom Duarte to become a most effective King from the moment he took the throne, in 1433. Considered to be one of the most educated medieval Kings, Dom João I wrote the *Livro da Montaria* (a book about hunting) which is a most valuable literary composition of the fifteenth century. He prepared in great detail an expansion plan for Portugal into North Africa and he conquered, having all his legitimate sons with him (Dom Duarte, Dom Pedro, Dom Henrique, Dom João and Dom Fernando), the city of Ceuta in 1415. That's why King Dom Duarte was referred in History as King of Portugal, of Algarve *and ruler of Ceuta.*

João Preto, my first known ancestor—I should say Dom João Preto—also went with King Dom João I and participated in this conquest.

Ruy de Pina (b. 1440 - d. 1522) was a chronicler, *Chronista Moor de Portugal e Guarda Moor da Torre do Tombo,* paid by the Portuguese

[24]

Crown to write the chronicles of several Kings of Portugal, namely Dom Duarte. In a very small chapter, Ruy de Pina wrote:

Das feiçooes corporaaes, virtudes e custumes d'ElRey Dom Duarte
*El Rey Dom Duarte foi homem de boa statura do corpo, e de **grandes e fortes membros**: tynha o acatamento de sua presença muy gracioso, os cabellos corredios, ho rostro redondo, os olhos molles, e pouca barba; foi homem desenvolto e **custumado em todalas boas manhas**, que no campo, na Corte, na paz e na guerra a hum perfeito Principe se requeressem: cavalgou ambalas sellas da brida, e **de gineta melhor que nenhuu de seu tempo**: foy muy humano a todos, e de boa condiçam: prezou-se em sendo **mancebo de boõ lutador**, e assy o foy, e folgou muito com os que em seu tempo bem o faziam: **foi caçador**, e monteiro, **sem myngoa nem quebra do despacho, e avyamento dos negocios necessarios**: foi homem allegre e de gracioso recebimento: foi Principe muy Catholico e amigo de Deos...foi muy piadoso e **manteve muy inteiramente sua palavra como scripta verdade**: amou muito a justiça: foi homem sesudo e de claro entendimento, **amador de sciencia de que teve grande conhecimento**, e nom per descurso d'Escollas, mas **per continuar d'estudar**, e leer per boõs livros...foi, e **naceo natural eloquente**, porque Deos ho dotou pera ysso com muitas graças: no comer, e dormir foi muy temperado, e assy **dotado de todalas perfeiçõoes do corpo e d'alma.***

What follows are the most relevant aspects of his description of Duarte, which translate as follows:

Das feiçooes corporaaes, virtudes e custumes d'ElRey Dom Duarte: "about the physical charactheristics, virtues and habits of King Dom Duarte." *grandes e fortes membros:* "...big and strong arms and legs." *custumado em todalas boas manhas:* "...skilled in all the valuable arts." *de gineta melhor que nenhuu de seu tempo:* "...no one could match him when riding on a 'gineta' saddle." *mancebo de boõ lutador:* "...he was a good wrestler during his youth." *foi caçador:* "...he was a good hunter." *sem myngoa nem quebra do despacho, e avyamento dos negocios necessaries:* "...but never forgetting the responsibilities of his position." *manteve muy inteiramente sua palavra como scripta verdade:* "...he always kept his word...there was never any need to have it in writing." *amador de sciencia de que teve grande conhecimento...per continuar d'estudar:* "...great scientific knowledge obtained through a permanent study." *naceo natural eloquente:* "...born with the gift of eloquence." *dotado de todalas perfeiçõoes do corpo e d'alma:* "...perfect of body and soul."

King Dom Duarte (b. 1391 – d. 1438)

King Dom Duarte's cognomen was "The Eloquent." One of his first decisions as King was to have *Cortes* sessions in the city of Santarém to get decisions on three main subjects:

• To restructure the civil service organization

• To produce a compilation of all the kingdom's existent laws

• To take measures to recover the wealth of the Crown

This last objective was achieved with the promulgation in the following year (1434) of the *Lei Mental*; basically, only a first male son (if there was one) could inherit, after the death of his father, any lands, real estate and values given by the Crown to the deceased as recognition of his services. If the deceased's first son was not a male, everything was to be returned to the Crown. I believe this shows by way of example how well prepared was King Dom Duarte for his position of King of Portugal and how seriously he took it.

I am just to address one additional subject that was of the utmost importance for Portugal, for Dom Duarte's brotherhood and for himself. For several years, his brothers Dom Henrique and Dom

Fernando (supported by the other two brothers, Dom Pedro and Dom João) pressed him to authorize the attempt to conquer the city of Tangier in the North of Africa (adding it to the city of Ceuta).

After having resisted that pressure during two years, Duarte finally authorized it in 1437 (and it was a decision he was to regret for the rest of his life). The mission was understaffed, under armed, badly implemented and it was a total disaster.

The Arabic army arrested Dom Fernando and the condition for his release was the return of the city of Ceuta to Arab control. There were two main factions in Portugal (even inside the inner royal family) and Dom Fernando died in the Tangier prison early in 1438 before any decision could be taken.

It is generally accepted that King Dom Duarte died of a plague (in September of 1438) but many say that after the death of his brother Dom Fernando, and the voluntary isolation of his brother Dom Henrique from a normal life (living in reclusion in *Sagres*, the South Western corner of Europe), Dom Duarte was never again the same person and had lost the will to live. Tragedy had dismantled one of the greatest royal families that ever existed in Portugal.

These events, dramatic as they were, give even more value to Dom Duarte's determination to go on writing and finish his book (which he was unable to accomplish). Duarte was actively writing this book at time of his death in 1438, even as his family and its aspirations were in shambles.

The Jews in Portugal

Due to their importance in the history of our Portugal it makes sense to spend some time describing the most important aspects of the Jews in Portugal (some of them not very pleasant, unfortunately).

There were various Jewish communities in the territory before Portugal existed as a kingdom (or even as an independent country). There were major Jewish communities with synagogues and all their specific life costumes and characteristics in several areas of the territory, namely in Santarém and Lisboa.

As an example of their importance in the fight against the Arabs, their rabbi Iáhia Aben-Yaisch was armed as a Knight in 1148 by the first Portuguese King Dom Afonso Henriques, and many Jewish communities were given royal written documents giving them lands and ensuring their safety.

It is believed that they lived in peace under royal protection until King Dom Dinis (b. 1261- d.1325). Problems related to usury (complaints from the Christian population) and the fact that the Catholic Church was not properly pleased with their economic importance in the country life made the co-existence of the two communities progressively more difficult. But by the fourteenth-century there remained tens of important Jewish communities spread all over Portugal (from Bragança in the North East, to Lagos in the South West). Unfortunately, there was an evident deterioration in the relations between Jews and the Christian population. As an example, King D. Pedro I (b. 1320 – d. 1367) signed in 1366 a royal decree forbidding Christians to enter the Jewish residential areas.

Throughout the years there were many other decrees, some in favor but most against Jewish interests. For example: in 1390, King Dom João I signed a decree (following on King Dom Dinis in 1279) forcing Jews to wear a badge (a 6-pointed red star, but not a yellow one); in 1403, he signed another decree forbidding Jews to carry weapons but simultaneously ruling that they could not be called by any Court or Authority on any Saturday.

In 1492, the Catholic Kings of Castile and Aragon (Spain) signed a decree expelling all Jews from their Kingdoms within four months (the consequence of an eventual refusal was a swift death penalty). Between 100,000 and 150,000 Jews entered in Portugal, authorized by King Dom João II (1455-1495); they could stay there for up to eight months but had to pay a certain price per head, unless they were rich and could buy out their freedom within the Portuguese kingdom with periodic donations to the Crown.

In 1496, King Dom Manuel I, under political pressure from the Kings of Castile and Aragon (but simultaneously not wanting to lose all the money the Jewish community represented for the Portuguese Crown) signed an astonishing decree. Its main points were:

• There were no more Jews in Portugal (they ceased to exist by decree)

• There were Old-Christians and "New-Christians"

• Baptism was forced upon the "New-Christian" babies

• "New-Christians" could not leave Portugal by sea. As they could not re-enter in Spain, they were confined to Portuguese lands and had to appear to convert themselves to Christianity, practicing their beliefs in secret, like the first Christians in the Roman Empire.

• Synagogues became Churches

• No religious prosecutions during 20 years

But the relationship between Old and New Christians was a lost cause. In 1506, only in Lisbon, 2,000 "New Christians" were killed in riots.

Let me give you another example (simultaneously dramatic and anecdotic): Estremoz is a city to the east of Lisbon in the Alentejo province, known for its clay artifacts; but it was dangerous to have them at home because there was the possibility to be accused of being Jew. Why? Many of these artifacts represented animals, namely bulls; at the time, the Portuguese word for the female bull was *toura* and its pronunciation was almost like *Torah*, the Pentateuch (the Jewish "bible").

By 1684, the "Saint Catholic Inquisition," which existed legally in Portugal by 1536, "purified" by fire more than 1,379 "New Christians."

A last comment about this theme: The real strength of a country depends, among other things, on the balance among social and ethnic groups. The weaknesses shown by the Portuguese Crown and its inability to fix these cultural and religious problems is considered by many as one of the most important reasons why Portugal lost its independence to Castile in 1581.

The Second Political Crisis in Portugal

In 1580, the situation in Portugal, as far as the Crown was concerned, was confused. A very young king, Dom Sebastião (the 16th King of Portugal) died in 1578 during a lost battle in the North of Africa (in Alcacer Quibir), leaving no sons. King *Cardinal* Dom Henrique (the 17th King of Portugal and uncle of Dom Sebastião), reigned from 1578 until is death, in the last day of January of 1580. King *Abbot* Dom António (the 18th King of Portugal and grand-son of King Dom Manuel I, the 14th King of Portugal) reigned from June to August of 1580.

Taking advantage of the clear existent confusion and weakness in the Portuguese society, King Dom Filipe II of Spain (Castile) who was son of Dª Isabel, a daughter of Dom Manuel I (the 14th King of Portugal) took over the country and became the 19th King of Portugal (Dom Filipe I of Portugal). He reigned from 1581 to 1598. So, from 1581 onward, the Kingdom of Spain (Castile) owned Iberia. King Dom Filipe III of Spain, became King Dom Filipe II of Portugal and reigned from 1598 to 1621. King Dom Filipe IV of Spain, became King Dom Filipe III of Portugal, reigning from 1621 to 1640.

Portugal regained its independence in 1640 and Dom João, the 8th Duke of Bragança (recall the earlier son of Dom João I, the 1st Duke of Bragança), became King Dom João IV of Portugal. There are a couple of questions that could be asked: Having in mind the power of Spain, how did Portugal get Castile (Spain) to let it go in 1640? How did was an heir to the Portuguese throne found after a 60 year break?

The answer might be presented in two parts:

1. The "war of the 30 years" between France and Spain (Castile) had the Cardinal Richelieu of France as the political mastermind. He sent messengers to Portugal and to Catalonia, offering support in various ways to organized uprisings. He also ensured that, as far as Portugal was concerned, France would recognize as King of Portugal, Dom João, the 8th Duke of Bragança! So, he really chose the next King of Portugal.

2. King Filipe IV of Castile refused to fight in more than one front simultaneously; so, he let Portugal go with it and ensured that he kept Catalonia; when the situation in Catalonia was fixed and the

30-years war was over, the situation in Portugal was so strongly consolidated by Dom João, the 8th Duke of Bragança (already King Dom João IV of Portugal) that it would take nothing less than a full scale war to reduce Portugal to submission again and the King of Castile did not consider he had the political conditions and support to keep his people at war.

This is why Portugal is an independent country and not a Spanish province like Galicia, Asturias, Navarre, Leon, Aragon and Catalonia, who also had been also independent Kingdoms. It was due to the political cunningness of Cardinal Richelieu of France and the intelligence of King Filipe IV of Castile!

Portuguese Chivalry & the Literary Record

I indulge myself taking the decision of spending some of your time — and patience — addressing a subject that I cherish very much and that could help us to forget some of the tragedies, negative and unpleasant events we have described so far. One of the most famous chivalric exploits from Duarte's time is the story of the "Twelve of England." I have done some research to elaborate on this legend, and I present it here for your consideration.

Late in the fourteenth century or early in the fifteenth century, twelve English ladies considered themselves insulted by twelve English knights and presented a formal complaint to the Duke of Lancaster. The Duke of Lancaster was the father-in-law of the Portuguese King Dom João I, and he asked Dom João I for help.

In due time, *eleven* Portuguese knights left by ship from Portugal's second major city, Porto, to fight in a joust the twelve English "naughty boys." We are told that the Portuguese won (honestly, I could not be sure about what this meant; they earned renown in the attempt, certainly). They returned back home after being honored by the delighted English ladies.

The most well known member of our "twelve good guys" is *Dom Alvaro Gonçalves Coutinho*, nicknamed *O Magriço* ("the thin one"). This gentleman did *not* take the ship to London with the other eleven but instead, went by land, through Spain, Burgundy, France and Flanders. There is a letter dated 26 December 1411, from the Duke of Burgundy and Earl of Flanders to our King Dom João I, thanking him for the services done to him by *O Magriço* and there is also documentation dated from 1599 with detailed description of the joust (see the reference in *Ruy de Pina – Chronica d'El-Rei D. Duarte* – Published by *Alfredo Coelho de Magalhães*).

Luis Vaz de Camões (b. 1524- d.1580) is considered to be the greatest Portuguese poet of all time. His most relevant work is *Os Lusíadas*, an epic poem of an enormous quality and dimension. This epic poem follows many of the literary specifics of the *Aeneid* (the major classic epic poem of Virgil, the greatest Roman poet; his original name was Publius Vergilius Maro, 70BC – 19 BC).

Os Lusíadas is divided in ten parts covering some of the more relevant facts of the history of Portugal (which is a major difference from the classic epic poems, as they do not cover real facts) using as background the detailed description of the discovery of the sea way to India; each part (named a *Canto*) has an average of one-hundred ten stanzas of eight lines each, and each line has exactly ten syllables. And of course, they rhyme.

The rhyme scheme is "ab ab ab cc" (the first, third and fifth line rhyme among them; the second, fourth and sixth line rhyme among them; the seventh and the eighth rhyme between them). As an example I offer, in modern Portuguese, the first stanza of *Os Lusíadas* (I must confess that I try not to feel a shiver going through my spine every time I read it, so emotionally strong it is):

[33]

As armas e os Barões assinalados

Que da ocidental praia lusitana

Por mares nunca dantes navegados

Passaram ainda além da Taprobana,*

Em perigos e guerras esforçados

Mais do que prometia a força humana

E entre gentes remotas edificaram

Novo reino que tanto sublimaram.

* *Taprobrana* is a XVI century name of an island in the Indic ocean

<u>The translation into English</u>:

The knights identified by their coats of arms

Who left Portugal from our western beaches

And sailing through seas never crossed before

Went beyond Taprobana,

Faced dangers and overcame great wars

Far beyond what was considered possible

And built among remote people

A new kingdom they so highly honored.

In the sixth *Cant,* there are twenty-five stanzas about "The Twelve of England"

(The Duke of Lancaster is therein named).

[34]

This is the kind of chivalric culture that Portugal was proud to present to the cultures of 14th and 15th century Europe. The influence of such cultures within Portugal is easy to see, from the unique rope-entwined Gothic architecture to the arms, armour and tactics of 14th century England and even the literary overlap.

Within Europe, the Knights of Portugal were highly regarded; and indeed influential enough that the jousting "tea" — the barrier between two mounted riders — adopted in Burgundy during the 15th century, appears to have been a Portuguese innovation.

Final Note to the Readers

King Dom Duarte of Portugal (1391 - 1438) died unexpectedly of a plague in August, 1438 leaving this book, which he dedicated to his wife Dª. Leonor, unfinished. Regrettably, he covered only seven of the total of sixteen themes he referred early in the book.

Dª. Leonor, a princess from Aragon (one of the Kingdoms of Iberia), became the Portuguese ruler at the time of Dom Duarte's death because their first son, later to be King Dom Afonso V of Portugal, was only six years old.

She signed all the official documents as "Leonor, the sad Queen" but not being Portuguese by birth and due to the increasing pressure from the people and from Dom Pedro (Dom Duarte's brother) she resigned in December 1440 and left Portugal taking with her all her personal belongings, including the *Livro da Ensinança de Bem Cavalgar Toda Sela* ("The Art of Riding on Every Saddle") and the *Leal Conselheiro'* ("Loyal Counselor").

Dª. Leonor left Portugal, heading first to Albuquerque (a town in Castile) then to Catalonia and finally to Naples (Italy). When King Charles VIII of France (1470 - 1498) conquered Naples in February of 1495, Dom Duarte's manuscripts were immediately integrated in the Blois Library and later on in the Royal Library of France (currently the French National Library in Paris, where they remain today).

Being a Portuguese national, proud of my heritage and ancestry, I consider this situation to be most unfortunate, to say the least.

Two editions have been produced based on the original manuscript and they were both used as sources in the translation done:

• *Typographia Rollandiana* published an exact printed copy of the original manuscript in 1843. This publication is in the Portuguese National Library in Lisbon and I went through it several times during the translation work to clear specific doubts.

• A critical edition from Mr. Joseph M. Piel was published in 1944. It includes a table of contents and some fifteen pages of a glossary with cross-references between certain words and terms. Mr. Piel has changed the spelling of many words, making them nearer to their current spelling — if they still exist in the current Portuguese language — and has also inserted appropriate punctuation whenever he felt the need for it; those decisions made the text much easier to understand.

My objective was to produce an accurate translation. I believe this translation reflects precisely my understanding of what King Dom Duarte wanted to convey to the readers of his book. I consider myself fully accountable for any deficiencies — for which I apologize beforehand — and I ask for your understanding. I did it to the best of my ability. Enjoy it!

António Franco Preto

This is the translation into English of the book of King Dom Eduarte[1] of Portugal (b.1391-d.1438)

---

[1] All the footnotes are the responsibility of the translators with one exception: the vast majority of the footnotes of the chapter XVI in Section 5—namely those with technical and historical content. They were written by Mr. Greg Mele. As far as the King's first name is concerned, please take note of two facts: First, in the XV century in Portugal all noblemen and squires were addressed with the prefix **Dom** to their first names as a sign of respect; later on, the prefix **Dom** was shortened to **D.** (Currently, it is very rare to find the prefix **Dom**; if there is any, **D.** is normally used). Second, the first name **Eduarte** ceased to exist in the Portuguese language, having been replaced by two first names: either **Eduardo** or **Duarte**; as history addresses **Dom Eduarte** (or **D. Eduarte**) as **D. Duarte**, we will use the this same first name (**Duarte**) throughout the whole book.

INTRODUCTION

In the name of Our Lord Jesus Christ, with His permission and benevolence and also of the Virgin Mary, His Holy Mother, Our Lady: This is the beginning of the book of the teaching how to ride on every saddle, written by King Dom Duarte of Portugal, of Algarve, and Ruler of Ceuta, who started this book when he was still an *Infante*.[2]

In the name of Our Lord Jesus Christ: Having in mind that we should be able to do everything, and in accordance with the saying that writing books is an endless task, which I do for my own relaxation and entertainment, and being aware that the art of being a good horseman is one of the main skills necessary to knights and squires, I am going to write several things about it with the objective of improving the riding skills of those who decide to read my writings in good will and to follow my recommendations. First of all be aware that these skills are easier gained by natural talent or vocation, and by having good horses, and by the continuous practice of riding, and by residing in houses and lands where there are good horsemen who are well esteemed because of that skill, rather than by knowing all about what I am writing and being unable to write additional recommendations and not continuously practicing the art, based on all the extant recommendations. But I do this to teach the ones less qualified and to enable the knowledgeable ones to remember the recommendations they agree with and to warn the others about the corrections they consider should be made to my recommendations. And the ones who want to acquire this art

---

[2] Prince (and heir apparent).

need to have the three main things that are necessary to acquire any other type of art: a strong will, sufficient power, and great knowledge. I will approach separately each one of the three, saying what I think appropriate, and even if we cannot really teach about power and will because they are achieved more by nature and special talent for each rather than through teaching, I am writing about them to arouse your interest and to show the power that we are generally able to achieve, if we have enough will and knowledge.

About my decision to write this book: some said I shouldn't spend the time doing it taking into consideration the many and great responsibilities I have; over and above that, it is also their opinion that each and everyone of us is able to learn this art by himself, so it is not necessary to write about it. My answer is that it is my wish to be able to offer others the possibility of acting in accordance with the rules, methods and the objectives I describe in the book. Considering what I read about the human heart, it is similar to the water-mill's stone, always in movement due to the driving water power, transforming grain into flour. The heart that in this manner wishing to be fulfilled, to receive good care from its owner, must sometimes have moments of unrestrained enjoyment, if there is the space and the time for it, as the heart might otherwise become ill-natured, which is the source of all wickedness. Feeling this way the brave Emperor Julius Caesar always took care, even if overburdened, to study and to write, whenever he had the opportunity. My heart cannot always get what is better and more beneficial for it, because some days I am living in the wilderness, hunting up hill and down dale, or the members of my council do not get to me early enough and I become idle; even with enough bodily activity, I am unable to spend the time available in activities that could bring me some merit as I am forced to spend time doing things I dislike.

I found good and beneficial relief and medicine from time to time, to thinking and writing by my own hand according to the interest and enjoyment I feel in so doing; otherwise I would not do it, as I am fully aware how much to do it or not means to me.

To those who say that this art does not need a book to be learned, I say that that is true. But I believe that the vast majority will find it beneficial to carefully read everything I am going to write. And because I do not know of anyone else who has written anything about this subject, I am pleased to write about this science, including several subjects that belong to our customs, although not completely within the normal scope of this science, since that will be beneficial to some, that others consider to be an excessive extension. And I know that the individual knowledge about one specific art might not be great, as a scattered virtue is weaker than a consolidated one, but conversation among people of various ranks and knowledge, some better than others, and with a normal level of understanding, should enable them to attain a fair knowledge: nevertheless as I have listened a great deal and my level of understanding is good, I strongly desire to write about this art, because the result might be good teaching with no disadvantages.

Those who want to learn the right way should start reading small sections, slowly and with great concentration, going back a couple of times to what they have already read to better learn it. If they read for long periods and very fast as if it was a storybook, they will loose the pleasure and become bored, because their level of understanding and recollection will not be that great; as a general rule this is the way to read a book of science or instruction.

FIRST PART: about the WILL

Chapter I is about the reasons why knights and squires should be skilled horsemen, due to the advantages and honor that such skill ensures

Since all men naturally value their honor, benefits and contentment, I am sure that all knights and squires should want very strongly to excel in the art of riding, as they will be well esteemed because of such a skill. Speaking about honor and benefits, it would take too much time to number how many men, during the wars of the king, (my lord and father whose soul rests with God), and in other wars, achieved great fame — status and benefits — due to their skills in this art. And this is true because one of the main things that helps more those who participate in wars, is to be a skilled horsemen. And we can really understand the great advantage that the skilled horsemen have when at war, compared to others less qualified in the art of riding, even if they have identical abilities in the other necessary arts; riding skills are one of the most valuable skills for warriors. And those who have good horses can get very little advantage out of them if they do not really have the appropriate riding skills, as they would not know how to do it. There are horsemen who are very skilled on a specific saddle whereas they are unable to maintain those skills on other saddles. And there are those who, if seen by connoisseurs just riding at a gallop wearing normal clothes, are judged not to be skilled horsemen. But when combating duly armored in jousts[3] against other riders, using a spear as the weapon, could not be criticized at all. And there are those who gain great advantage over others on every maneuver, due to their natural talent and because they have had opportunities to learn and to practice frequently. But the knight or squire who knows little about riding should not be harshly judged by those who understand their shortcomings in this art, that is most helpful to those who really know it as it should be. This art brings, besides other advantages, courage to the heart. And this is proven by seeing weak-hearted youngsters and men who confess to not being able to do on foot what the good and brave do, but who when on a horse, if they are skilled in this art, show themselves to be strong-willed and to believe themselves able to gain advantage over other riders, equally strong-willed, but with little skill in riding. And this same change of attitude happens in many other situations of great importance during a war. Always to have good horses, to know them well and how to take care of them, improving their qualities and reducing their weak points, is worth more than knowing any other art imperfectly. And having the horses always available brings one great advantages, in honor and benefits, over others who don't. And this is considered to be so by those with great experience, who spend a great part of their lives at war. It is very well known by all of those who have been to war and seen and heard about great achievements, the advantages of having good horses and being a skilled rider. I won't write more about this to avoid spending too much time on it.

---

[3] Several times throughout the text I use the original Portuguese word *justas*.

Chapter II : about the advantages of being a skilled horseman in peacetime

In peaceful times those who are skilled horsemen have great advantage in jousts, in tournaments, playing with canes[4] , maneuvering and throwing spears. They hold the same advantage in all other dexterities performed in the course of riding that occurs frequently on the lords' estates. In those activities, since they have had the experience to overcome difficulties and troubles, the fact that they are skilled horsemen gives them advantages over others who face the same difficulties and troubles and have identical physical qualities, bu do not have the same riding skills. And to be very good at hunting up and down slopes, riding skills give them great advantages as they have the knowledge essential better to cope with collisions, to stay well poised on the horse and strong in the saddles enabling them better to strike with a weapon, as they know the limits their horses can endure and how to use them, simultaneously protecting themselves from many dangers. All these and other things that are going to be described in the THIRD PART are very much necessary to those who want to become good hunters. The lords greatly esteem those who are skilled horsemen and therefore have some basic qualities that are important in war

---

[4] Literally "jugar as canas," a game with reeds, possibly similar to the Northern European béhourd, where combatants used canes instead of swords to train for tournaments and war. Compare this with the ash/whalebone weapons found in the béhourd. The béhourd (German: behort/buhurt, Italian: bagordo) was a limited form of both mounted and foot tournament, initially fought as a training exercise by squires, or as a less formal (and thus less expensive) celebration-at-arms by nobles. The contests were conducted with blunted lances, sword-batons or whalebone swords, and armour of linen and *cuir-boulli* (hardened leather).

and other activities; it is also very important to the lords to have on their estates many good horses and skilled horsemen able to ride them well. It is also important for those who want to take employment for wages to show everywhere that they are knowledgeable in the equestrian arts, and be recognized as men able to perform important duties and to be trustworthy.

Chapter III: What can be said against the benefits of having riding skills and the rebuttal

We should not take in consideration those who say that—in their opinion—good horsemen should be esteemed just for having those skills; because this art in itself is not enough to make anyone to be considered as a person of great value, as it happens in other professions; as for example when they are brokers or someone who breeds horses for sale. The three things that lead men, by the grace of God, to achieve all the good during this life and in the next, are: to have the will to do everything virtuously and faithfully towards God and men; to have sufficient strength in their bodies and hearts to be able to do all difficult things and to oppose and cope with all adversities; and to be knowledgeable through experience of the things that belong to their status and professions, enabling them to act correctly in accordance with their objectives, to oppose when necessary and to overcome adversities. And these are the virtues that are sufficient to give great benefits to those who have them, and not other skills, unless they are combined with those virtues. But those who do not have those three virtues should not think that, just being skilled in riding, combat or dancing, would be enough to make them knights or squires; at best they could be servants or buffoons. And those who have these three main virtues would be as good as they are virtuous. And it would help them to gain additional skills in other arts. And all should work hard to maximize their virtues, in accordance to their status, age and temper, due to the great benefits, relaxation and enjoyment that those virtues bring to the ones that know how to use them with the aptitude they have and in the appropriate circumstances.

Chapter IV: About the recreation that this art provides

Much recreation and relaxation of spirit are surely enjoyed by those who are well skilled in the art of riding. We say this because we see how they are praised for the advantages they have by those who are skilled only in activities that provide almost no benefits at all, like throwing the iron bar, doing double leg jumps and similar things. If those who throw the iron bar and do double leg jumps get enjoyment out of these abilities, we can imagine the recreation and relaxation of spirit enjoyed by the skilled horse riders, an art that has such a privileged place. It is also well known that good horses bring happiness to the hearts of the riders, if they are at least reasonably skilled. So, I conclude: considering the praises received and the recreation enjoyed by those who are skilled riders, and many other consequences, it is only natural that these skills are sought after by so many. And I have just written so much about this to motivate the readers to have a strong will to learn about the art of riding; that will be sufficient to easily achieve the power and the knowledge necessary to become good horsemen. In summary, a man with good horses who knows how to ride them well, has seven advantages:

First — readiness to assist his master, taking care of many duties that will bring him much honor and benefits

Second — to be at ease

Third — to be respected

Fourth — to be protected

Fifth — to be feared

Sixth — to be light-hearted

Seventh — to have a bigger and better heart[5]

And we understand that these advantages are greater for them than for those with bad horses and weak riding skills; nevertheless, there are other things that can provide the advantages referred above. Besides all these, we very much praise this art because a healthy man, with strong will, if he does not get fat, is able to keep his skills as he ages, which does not happen with most arts. And those who want to have some advantage over others should be able to achieve that through riding a horse or any other quadruped reasonably trained.

This is the end of the **FIRST PART**, about the **WILL** and the beginning of the **SECOND PART**, about the **POWER**

---

[5] In the original, D. Duarte mentions six advantages a man with good horses who knows how to ride them well, has, but he describes seven. I have made the due correction.

SECOND PART — About POWER

Chapter I — The power of the body and the power of wealth

In what concerns the power every horsemen should have, we consider it divided in two parts: the power of the body and the power of wealth. In what concerns the power of the body some think that due to their physical weakness, old age or obesity, they are unable to become good horsemen and they lose the will to learn those things which are necessary to do this. They are totally wrong, not only relative to the art of riding but also to all the other good things that they can still learn if they keep their will and hope. And they can stay away from that error if they take the following precaution: those who have doubts about the possibility of becoming good horsemen due to their physical weakness, old age or any other reason would easily find others who became good horsemen even though they were weaker and older. And this happens to the majority of men facing their limitations, if they have any; they can always find others with greater limitations who yet are not effectively restrained by them, and are therefore able to gain advantages from the art they pursue. And seeing others that, being in the same situation and even with more physical restrictions, are reasonable horsemen, they should understand that if they keep a strong will and a determination to learn, the power of their bodies will be sufficient, as it has been for others. And I think that if everybody maintains a strong determination and will, only very few would not be able to become reasonable horsemen through lack of the minimal physical conditions. I am not saying that everybody could become a very good horseman as I am sure that in the whole

[50]

world there are not many with all the necessary qualities — which I will have the opportunity to describe later — to be an exceptional horseman. But it would be enough that, when riding beasts, they behave like men and not like beasts[6].

Chapter II — The power of wealth

The power of wealth is divided in two parts: first, to choose and buy good beasts; then, the ability to take care of them. And to have these kinds of wealth, a strong will and knowledge are sufficient in most cases; only very few would not have the sufficient power required to be able to fulfill their objectives in this area. If the gamblers find opportunities and ways to gamble, if the hard drinkers find money to buy wine and if the same happens to others with other most unfortunate habits that are very much censured and not favored by the lords, we say that determination and will should enable those who need to buy and to take care of horses, to find a solution. Because there is no objective that the lords are more accustomed to protect, support and favor; therefore, it should constitute no embarrassment to those who need it, to ask them for help.

Knowledge helps power, enabling the buyer to get good colts and to refuse others that are too expensive. And being knowledgeable, one can buy horses, improve their qualities and value and use them with advantages that others could not, for lack of knowledge. And

---

[6] For the first time in the book D. Duarte plays on words. In this sentence, he uses the same word (*besta*) to name the horse and the horseman (*besta* for beast and *besta* also for a stupid and brutish person). Usually he is a very polite writer. He wanted very much to make a point! It is also interesting to note that D. Duarte uses throughout his book either the word *cavalo* (horse) or the word *besta* (beast) when referring to a horse.

the same happens in regard to caring for them; it will be much cheaper for those who know how to do it and have strong determination than for the ones who are not knowledgeable. And I am not going to talk about the ways to take good care of the beasts during winters and summers, putting weight on them, the knowledge of their diseases, breeding and the training process from a young age, because all these needs are described in detail in some veterinary books. But those who are determined and are knowledgeable about these things, if they are not unfortunate with the beasts, will always be better able than others to have good beasts and to be able to take good care of them.

THIRD PART: XVI Main Recommendations for the Skilled HORSEMEN

Here starts the THIRD PART, in which XVI MAIN · RECOMMENDATIONS are given to skilled horsemen.

Introduction:

Having finished the first two parts: the first one about the reasons why knights and squires should be determined to become skilled horsemen, the second one about the power of the body and the power of wealth—that the majority have in sufficient quantity—I am going to write the THIRD PART, in which I am going to give what recommendations I can, to enable the readers to acquire the extensive knowledge they need to become good horsemen. And because it is impossible to describe how certain things are practiced, so they are shown by example, it will be the responsibility of the readers who do not understand my writing to question those they know to be knowledgeable; they will teach them everything they are unable to learn by themselves. It is necessary to know that a skilled horseman should have the following qualities[7]:

---

[7] Out of the numbered sixteen sections of the book's THIRD PART (the main part of the book representing around ninety percent of the total number of pages) D. Duarte only wrote seven (the first six plus the eighth, which he numbered as the seventh). It is therefore clear that D. Duarte died unexpectedly (from a plague) before having had the possibility to finish the book; I also believe that he had no time to make revisions to most of the written chapters. Assuming that the unwritten chapters would have had the same average length as the written ones, I would say that the book was not more than half finished (even so, I consider that the most

1. The most important of all — to stay firmly mounted on the beast in everything you do and also no matter what might happen to you.

2. Not to fear falling off the beast or with her, keeping the appropriate confidence in yourself, the beast and the terrain where you are riding, to do whatever would be necessary.

3. To be safe with determination and bodily composure in everything you need to do, giving the impression of safety with your bearing.

4. To be quiet on the saddle in a reasonable manner, in accordance to the needs required by the beast's behavior.

5. To be at ease in every action; I will make briefly, as well as I possibly can, some recommendations regarding several tricks one could use when riding.

6. To know how to use the spurs according to the moment and to the beast; I will describe how the spurs should be and how could we use a wooden stick or a staff to control the beast.

---

important matters D. Duarte want to convey to the readers were written). It is also important to note that sometimes D. Duarte uses the word *senhores* to address wealthy people (to whom, for example, a horseman asks employment for wages or money to be able to buy horses and take care of them); they are not necessarily noblemen, otherwise D. Duarte would have addressed them as such; but I have no doubts they were wealthy, owning land and houses; as I did not find a better solution I have decided to use the word lords as a translation into English for the original word *senhores*.

7. To handle the bridle[8] and the beast's mouth with attention at all times.

8. To know how to protect yourself from many dangers such as trees falling down, other men and beasts, as the lack of these skills result many times in disasters.

9. To know how to overcome the hazards of riding everywhere, namely through woods, mountains and passes.

10. To be wise in everything you do when riding.

11. To be elegant on the saddle and when riding, according to the beast's reactions. And to know how to correct yourself and the beast in order to look good, disguising difficulties whenever necessary.

12. To be determined to endure long journeys and tough gallops saving, as much as possible, the beast's efforts and your own.

13. To know well your beast's mouth using appropriately made to measure bridles.

14. To know the beast's limitations and flaws and to be able to reduce or correct them.

15. To be aware of, to keep and to improve your own skills, not losing them by disordered behavior or due to lack of will to go on learning.

16. To be aware, through experience and knowledge of the general principles, of your own qualities and skills required for every needs you might have. Many more things are necessary to know to be a

---

[8] In the Portuguese language we have the word *freo* (always used by the author) for both **bridle** and **bit**; I have translated it always as "bridle" (even accepting that many times it is just the **bit**; but we know that the **bit** does not work without being assembled in the horse's headgear).

perfect horseman and they are described in the veterinary books; but as I do not want to prolong this introduction and others will write about them, and I do not have so much experience about them as I have about the things I am writing about, I have decided not to discuss them; but to those who are going to read the books, I say that their master's skills in riding would surely be improved by the knowledge they acquire reading about this science.

Section 1 — About being STRONG

Chapter I - About being firmly mounted on the beast in everything you do and no matter what might happen to you[9]

I have mentioned before that one of the main qualities of a good horseman was to be strongly mounted on the beast. There are six things that help you to achieve that:

1. To stay firm and erect on the saddle in everything you do

2. To press your legs against the beast

3. To have your feet firm[10] in the stirrups

4. To know how and when to use your hands

---

[9] Once again, D. Duarte repeats himself.

[10] In the Portuguese language we have only the word *firme* for both "firm" and "steady" (D. Duarte writes always, *pees firmes nas estrebeiras*); I have used— almost always—the word **firm** as the translation for *firme* even accepting that in some specific situations the word **steady** looks to be more appropriate.

5. To know the best way to ride, specific to each saddle, in accordance to its type and preparation, in order to stay mounted as strongly as possible

6. To know how to correct yourself, the saddle, and the stirrups better to manage every action you need to take, in accordance with the beast's behavior

All these things are important and we should be able to use them, not all in the same way, not always and not with all beasts. Because the main ones and the most general, are: the knowledge required to stay firm and erect in everything you do when mounted on the beast; the leg's pressing against the beast; the help of the feet and hands; the knowledge of the various types of saddles; your own preparation, the preparation of the saddles and of the stirrups.

Chapter II — About "Bravante" saddles

In order to be crystal clear on the subject, it is necessary to know that there are five different styles of riding correctly and that all the others are derived from these five.

First — There are the saddles which require the legs to stay extended, a little bit forward with the feet firm on the stirrups; all these things to be done in such a way that a good balance is obtained not paying more attention to the steadiness of the feet on the stirrups, than to the pressing of the legs on the beast or to the way you are seated on the saddle; equal attention should be given to each one of the three to enable you to get the benefits you can take out of each one of them. The saddles used in our land that require this style of riding are currently known as "Bravante," as well as others of similar types (as far as the riding style is concerned). In all of them, the style which keeps you strongly mounted is the following: to lengthen the stirrup straps up to the point that enables you to stay firm on them with your legs extended. This means that it is necessary to feel your feet steady on the stirrups without loosening your legs. But, as I wrote before, you should pay equal attention to the steadiness of your feet on the stirrups, to the pressing of your legs on the beast and to the way you are seated on the saddle.

Chapter III—About those who do not pay great attention to the stirrups

Second—This style is based on staying seated on the saddle, with your legs extended or a bit flexed, not paying great attention to the stirrups leather strap length, in such a way that your feet are not firm on the stirrups. This style is used, as far as I was told, in England and in several Italian counties, where the saddles used are of different types. And the strength of this style of riding is based mainly on keeping the body erect on the saddle and pressing the legs—extended and maintaining a straight line with the body— against the beast, not paying great attention to the stirrups.

Nevertheless, in my opinion, even considering the different types of the saddles they use and their specific needs, the help which one can get from the stirrups should not be completely forgotten; but I understand why horsemen using this style of riding pay more attention to the pressing of their legs against the beast and to the upright position of their bodies—because that is how they know to ride and to react correctly to the beast's behavior—rather than to the help they could get from their feet on the stirrups.

Chapter IV—About those who ride firm and erect on the stirrups

Third—This style is based on riding firm on the stirrups with the legs extended and not being seated on the saddle, but having the body balance helped by the saddle-bows: the pommel and the cantle[11].

Those who use this riding style have learned it in the old times. And in tournaments and in jousts and in other similar situations, the correct style of riding is the following: to equip the horse in such a way that the stirrups stay fixed to the horse's body using an additional system of interlaced ropes (tying the stirrups together underneath the horse's belly) or by any other appropriate system. They—the stirrups—should be in such a position that the horseman's legs stay extended straight down and not even slightly forward. And the feet are to stay very firm on the stirrups and you are to never be seated on the saddle, as that would result in loss of elegance, loss of agility and loss of body quietness and would make you less strong. And no one should think that he could become stronger in jousts if he decides to keep even one of his legs a bit flexed because it would certainly produce the contrary; with the stirrups well fixed to the horse's body you should keep your legs extended straight down because that's the best way of avoiding defeats and falls from the horse and it will also give your riding additional elegance and handsomeness.

---

[11] Pommel—upward projecting front part (bow) of saddle; Cantle—hind-bow of saddle.

Chapter V—About those who ride with flexed legs

F*ourth*—This style of riding is based on keeping the legs always flexed, staying well seated on the saddle and with both feet firm on the stirrups as it was referred for the Bravante saddles and others that require a similar riding style; the difference being that in this style the legs are to be kept always flexed and not extended as in the riding style used with Bravante saddles. These saddles—and others that require the same riding style—are called "Gineta"[12] saddles.

And the best way to ride using this style is to keep your legs and feet pressed against the horse's body as much as you can, staying seated always in the center of the saddle, leaning neither towards the pommel nor towards the cantle. And your feet should stay firm on the stirrups with the heels well down, keeping your body well balanced on the saddle, never easing the pressure of your legs against the horse's body and also never losing the firmness of your feet on the stirrups. However, you should not press your feet too strongly against the stirrups to avoid raising your body from the saddle or losing the pressure of your legs against the horse's body, and you also should not press your legs too strongly against the horse's body, to avoid losing the firmness of your feet on the stirrups. And you should press your thighs, your knees and your calves equally against the horse's body to stay mounted on the horse as strongly as you possibly can. And your specific position on the saddle should vary in accordance to the beast's movements. If the beast is jumping, you should keep your body in the center of the

---

[12] The "Gineta" saddles and riding style were brought to us by the Arabs from he North of Africa and the horseman's weight is totally supported by the saddle and not by the stirrups.

saddle, firming your feet on the stirrups and pressing your legs against the horse's body, inclining your body backwards, as it will be described later on when I will discuss the actions horsemen should take not to fall down forward. And if the beast is trotting well your best action is to have your body firm and near the cantle. And if the beast is either galloping or trotting badly or at a fast pace, you should raise yourself a bit on the stirrups and get your body nearer to the pommel.

Regarding all the types of saddles already mentioned it is possible to ride on them with the legs flexed as in Gineta saddles and to stay strong, calm and at ease; but, as far as elegance is concerned, I choose those who ride erect on Gineta saddles.

Chapter VI — About riding with no saddle at all or just with a saddlecloth

Fifth — This is about riding with no stirrups and just with a saddlecloth or even without it. To master this, you depend on your skills in pressing your legs against the beast and your ability to stay erect. And there are three different ways to do it: First, with your legs extended and pressing the beast's body with your thighs and knees.

Second, with your legs flexed as much as possible, pressing them against the beast's body.

Third, pressing your legs against the beast's body and your tip toes against or — if possible — underneath the beast's belly.

Chapter VII—Advantages of knowing all these styles of riding

All the other styles of riding are based on the five already described. And I have seen each one of them being used in a good manner by those who know which is the most appropriate style to be used in accordance to the saddle and the beast they have; there are others who, knowing only one style of riding, have to use it in every circumstance, without regard to the saddle they have. But those who want to become good horsemen should know as much as possible about all these riding styles, because they might need to use any one of them, for various reasons: one's stirrup strap might break, the straps might be too long or too short without it being possible to correct them, or the saddles available might be of different types. And if he knows but one riding style he might be worth less than half a man. And there are many recognized as horsemen who admit that, if their stirrup strap happens to break they would be unable to do more than just basic things on the horse; otherwise they could get themselves into very dangerous situations. And others, knowing how to ride using various styles, would not be too concerned. And I think that if we were to ask a *Marim*[13] from Fès to ride a horse using a Bravante saddle with long stirrups straps he would not be neither at ease nor a good rider, even if he is a qualified horseman using a Gineta saddle. I also do not believe that an Englishman or a Frenchman could ride a horse reasonably well using a Gineta saddle with short stirrups straps, if they had no previous experience on it. And these type of situations will happen

---

[13] *Marim* — a specific military (or also a civilian?) position among the Arabs of the North of Africa. At the time, Fès was the most important city of that area of the North of Africa (currently Morocco).

to any who only know one riding style; they will be half paralyzed if they are given a type of saddle which they do not know how to ride on; and that will not happen to a good horseman; on the contrary, in times of need, a good horseman, unlike the others, does not get too concerned with the model of saddle or with the stirrups he might be forced to use.

Chapter VIII — Why it is always best to ride erect no matter what the beast does and the various ways we can fall down

In order to stay strongly mounted using any riding style it is mainly necessary to stay erect on the saddle no matter what the beast does, to know where we can get help from and what should we do in every situation. And the outcome depends on what we do. And to stay erect, the following should be understood: we can only be thrown out in four directions — forward, backward and to either side of the beast.

I can be thrown off forward if the beast stops quickly on its fore feet, or bucks its front feet landing them back in the same place as some beasts do out of malice, or bucking on all feet simultaneously, putting the head between the front feet when landing[14], or running in a disordered way, or jumping in an unexpected way and throwing itself impetuously into a ravine, a ditch or any other similar uneven ground, or stumbling over any obstacle when running, suddenly stopping on its front feet without falling.

I can be thrown off backwards if the beast rears up, bucks or jumps at the starting of the run, if it gallops very fast up a slope without

---

[14] Crow hopping, a form of bucking.

warning, or through dense woodland rendering difficult my body movements and causing me to fall. I can be thrown off on either side by a skittish horse who turns fast and unexpectedly to one of its sides, clockwise or counter-clockwise, or moves the shoulders in an unusual way, or bucks and simultaneously kicks out or stops abruptly and changes direction at the same time. I can also be thrown off to any of the four directions due to a collision or attack, or maneuvering or throwing a spear, or striking with a sword, or due to any other movement that I have not mastered well enough to avoid falling down as a consequence of my body movements and through my own fault, without having any reason to put the blame on the beast.

Chapter IX—How best to avoid being thrown over the beast's head

Relative to all the various ways we can be thrown off the beast, we have great advantages if we know how to stay erect on the saddle; you will quickly see that not mastering this requirement is the main reason why most horsemen fall down. If the beast I am riding stops quickly on its forehand, I have to protect myself from falling off forward and it is natural that, instinctively, I will grab the horse's mane with my hands and simultaneously lean my body forward which in reality would help the beast to throw me off over its head. As a matter of fact you should not do that—unless you lack the required knowledge—because in all the situations that might have as a consequence you be thrown off forward, the help of your hands is not efficient and they should not be used except as a last resort, when you are already falling down; or, as it has sometimes happened, when the beast has short hopped and landed with the front feet extended and a bit forward, I have with one hand grabbed the cantle or an iron support some saddles have on the rear and I have stayed firm on the saddle, being able to keep my body erect, while refraining from grabbing the mane with my hands. And those who know to do this are able to hide the problem from others — even if they carry a short wooden stick in the hand — if they are dressed appropriately. And I found this solution very effective for me, having done it without hearing or being told about it. And I believe it could be very helpful, in times of need, to those who decide to use it; but it should be avoided as much as possible. But those who want to stay protected from all the beast's actions that could throw them off forward, must keep in their minds that they should press their legs against the beast, keep their feet firm on the stirrups and lean their bodies backwards as much as possible, keeping their legs extended or flexed in accordance with the saddle they use. And they can still get an additional advantage if they put their bodies in an oblique line relative to the beast's body, flexing one leg to better press it against the beast's body; this way, your body stays firmer and more secure on the beast. And doing as I said you should not have to deal with jolts sufficiently strong to unbalance you, causing great difficulties. Still, if the beast usually extends its front feet forward, you can correct that action just by firming your feet on the stirrups and keeping your body erect — and leaning it a bit backward if needed — without having the need to press your legs against the beast.

Chapter X — How best to avoid being thrown over the beast's back

Relative to everything the beast does to throw us off, all men take the best help they can which usually is to hold on tight to the beast using their hands and lean their bodies forward but they are wrong, because they should never use their hands to hold tight to the beast if they can solve their difficulties through the correct positioning of their bodies and pressing their legs against the beast's body. And we should avoid using our hands because it is not elegant and also because we should keep them free for as long as possible, enabling us to use them if and when we really need them; we should really try to stay mounted on the beast without the help of our hands. And if we do need to use them, better we grab the beast's mane or the pommel rather than the bridle. There are many men who, when the beast starts running, grab the mane with one or both hands in order to feel firm and calm, and they cannot avoid it because they are used to doing it. I have found a solution for them: they should not gallop on the beast for several days until they forget that habit, always keeping the right hand free. And when the horse starts rearing, they should put their bodies in an oblique position relative to the beast's body and lean forward. And that is the way it should be done to keep the beast's jolts from moving the horseman's body backwards; this way, the horseman is more firm on the horse that with the body erect, which is actually preferable to allowing the body to be moved backwards. And when I get my body erect, the beast's bucks have ended and the beast is in a normal gallop. And when that happens, the horseman feels himself secure and calm without the help of his hands. And relative to all the things that can throw us off backwards, we should mainly use — as our best help — the position of our body, the pressure of our legs against the beast's body and, in case of major need, our hands; our feet are of very little

[66]

use in this situation. In my opinion, we are more likely in this situation to fall down, because we have positioned ourselves very firmly on our feet, rather than to receive any real help from them. And I recommend that, whenever the beast goes up a slope, the rider should keep his body erect without grabbing the mane with his hands, should flex his legs, pressing them against the beast, and should raise his feet backwards; doing all these actions, the ground will look flatter than it really is, as experience will prove.

Chapter XI — Walking erect — analogies between riding and behavior in life[15],[16]

Having described various ways of achieving our objective of staying erect when mounted on the beast, we should also behave in life acting in such a way that we stay firmly mounted on it, not falling down due to the malice of many; this could happen whenever we see things that are opposed to what we have done or said, against things we care about and things dear to our memory, trying to destroy them in such a way that we feel nothing but anger, fury, hate, sadness, weakness in our heart, self-deprecation or ingratitude to God and men, causing loss of faith or despair, preventing us from going on and accomplishing the things we could and should do, or

---

[15] It is interesting to note that D. Duarte gives great importance to appearances; therefore, from time to time (and you will find that throughout the text) he approaches the best way to hide from others the actions required to overcome unexpected difficulties faced when riding. He also approaches the need to showing off several qualities such as elegance, strength, fearlessness, safety, calm and self control.

[16] D. Duarte copied this chapter later on into his book *Leal Conselheiro*, chapter 83.

laziness originating in the weakness and laxness of our will, when in reality what we should do is to keep hoping to receive the vital help from our Lord God, enabling us to straighten up using the necessary determination and the good advice of those who, having great knowledge and long and good experience, are able and willing to give us the good counsel we must be willing to accept to go on doing the things we should. And we should have in mind the actions and emotions opposite to those that would lead us to fall down, as we have already described. And we should go on mentioning and paying attention to those things that are a good medicine to fight all the weaknesses that are most dangerous to us and not pay attention, even if we so desire, to the things that would cause us to fall down; because if we are sad, we feel many times the desire to go on speaking about the things that are the cause of our sadness, ultimately increasing it. And if we use all our determination to do what we should be doing, with the grace of our Lord God, we will be able, with His help, to achieve what we really want.

And if presumptuousness, arrogance or vainglory threaten to cause our fall, making us forget some of the God-given principles that are good for soul and body, we must remember how little we are worth and how small is our power, having the awareness of our weaknesses and limitations, in order to be—through His grace—protected from making the errors already described. And if we do not feel in ourselves the necessary strength, we should ask the help of God—who gave us all good things—enabling us to go on doing what is right. And if we do not find that good advice leads to immediate success, we should persevere and we will see later the great benefits that we can get as a consequence of our determination and care.

And if we start doing a few things with good intentions and sound reasons and setbacks happen due to men's malice or to misfortune, we should never cease to act correctly in accordance with our needs, always fulfilling our commitments in the due time and never being too hasty in the things we have to do. But, if we maintain our will and determination without being upset, we will be able to act properly and when the time is right, in accordance to what each objective requires. And living our life in this way with the help of God — who gave us all good things — we will stay erect and light-hearted in all our doings. And it might seem that I have written too much about these subjects, and this may seem to be a digression. I did it because I am sure that this would bring benefits to some, even if others do not have the same opinion.

Chapter XII — What should we do to avoid falling to the ground

Relative to everything the beast does, as I already said, to throw us off in any direction, we receive the most important help from the correct positioning and movements of our body, neither too fast nor too slow, to avoid turning round before the beast does or to avoid keeping in the same position as the beast turns round or changes direction. But, through knowledge, principles of safety and practice, our body reacts in accordance to the beast's movements: if the beast turns round with its front feet high and hind legs low (rearing), we lean our body a bit forward and down; if the beast turns round on its front feet with its hind legs high (bucking), our body should stay erect, leaning a bit backwards in accordance to the beast's body position, neither after nor before the beast's movement. Acting correctly this way, we would neither fall nor get exposed. And it would help us if we press our legs against the horse's body additionally helping ourselves with our feet and hands, if circumstances require.

Chapter XIII — How best to press the legs against the horse and how best to place the feet

Coming back to our main subject, there are questions put by some about the best way to press the legs — if it is best to press the legs against the horse's body with the knees, with the thighs or with the leg's calves. And if it is best, in order to stay firm and strongly mounted, to have the feet totally inside the stirrups, by their middle or just by the toes.

To all this I say that there is not one technique better than the other two as I have seen good and strong horsemen using all of them. To be strongly mounted, everyone should use the way which fits him best, in accordance with the saddle and stirrups used and the beast's behavior. And not too much attention should be paid to which technique you use to press your legs against the beast's body or place your feet in the stirrups; because everybody knows that if you want to be strongly mounted when using a Gineta saddle it is necessary to press with your knees and knee-caps; and a good part of being strongly mounted on Gineta saddles comes from your heels and the spurs whereas your thighs are of very little importance. And the riders who use Bravante saddles get great help from their thighs. And all those who compete in our jousts also receive great help from their knees and knee-caps.

And the same happens with the placement of your feet in the stirrups; in accordance with our experience, some do it one way, some do it in another way. But in general, most feel strongly mounted when placing their feet totally inside the stirrups. And about all this, you should not forget my advice: if you want to place your feet totally inside the stirrups, in order to feel yourself very firm you should keep your toes out; if you place your feet inside the stirrups by their middle or just by the toes, then you should keep your toes in. And those who decide to try this technique will find that my advice is the right one and therefore they will not need to look for other reasons to do it the way I say.

And I am saying that you should not place your toes totally in or totally out but just enough for you feel more firm. And this placement technique of your feet has the objective of helping you to feel and stay strongly mounted; because, if your objective is to look good, then you should keep your feet straight on, with your toes neither in nor out.

Chapter XIV—Advantages of knowing the best way to ride on every type of saddle

It has already been described how we can help ourselves by a correct position of our body, by the pressing of our legs against the beast's body and by the firmness of our feet in the stirrups; the help we can get from our hands is nothing but a last resource, after every other solution has failed. And we should also consider the help we get from knowing the best way of riding on the saddle we are using and its preparation, the preparation of the stirrups and our own. And, as I said, we get advantages by knowing how best to ride on every type of saddle, for example, how and why a Bravante saddle requires our legs to stay flexed and our body firmly seated on it. And those who are used to ride on saddles requiring the legs to stay extended—like Bravante saddles—would never be able to ride with the legs extended on Bravante saddles as strongly as the ones who are used to ride with their legs flexed as required by these saddles. And the same happens with all the various types of riding; a man will never be a good horseman if he is not able to chose the most appropriate way of riding on every type of saddle. And, if he is a good horseman, he is able to choose the most appropriate way of riding on every type of saddle.

With Bravante' saddles, it is necessary to use various ways of riding in accordance with their various models; because there are some types[17] with high and strong pommels and cantles and narrow in the middle.

On this kind of saddle, the horseman should never try to ride the way he is used to, well seated in the middle of the saddle, because he will not be able to do it correctly if the beast becomes wild and hard to control. In this kind of saddle, the best solution for the rider is to keep himself very firm on the stirrups, with his legs extended, with his upper body two or three fingers above the saddle.[18] Contrarily, if the saddle is long and flat, the best way of riding is to stay firmly on the seat; nevertheless, he should not do it in such a way that it might result in losing the strength and aid which staying firm on his feet and pressing his legs against the beast's body gives him. And, as I wrote before, when competing in our jousts, if the stirrups are well fixed to the horse's body,[19] it is better to stay erect and high on the stirrups than to be seated on the saddle; if the stirrups are not fixed with the ropes, then, it is better to be seated on the saddle rather than high on the stirrups. So, we see that every type of saddle requires a specific way of riding—even that sometimes the differences among them are not that big.

---

[17] Bravante saddles

[18] Therefore, not being seated on the saddle at all.

[19] Using the additional system of interlaced ropes underneath the beast's belly to fix them.

[72]

Chapter XV—How to take care of the saddle, the stirrups, the bridle and all the other equipment, ensuring they are strong and have been correctly prepared, avoiding breakage or displacement from their correct positions

We must take good care of the saddle, the bridle and the stirrups, ensuring that they are strong, that they have the necessary resistance and are of good quality to avoid failure of any of them; otherwise, we might die, meet with an accident, or be shamed. And we will achieve this if we frequently check them and if we detect any problem, we fix it immediately, avoiding negligence and using all necessary means. And if those given that job and responsibility do not act as ordered, they should not avoid punishment; because there is nothing related to the preparation of the beast that should be more carefully checked than the saddle, the bridle and the stirrups. On this subject we should have in consideration advice I heard from our late King, my lord and my father, whose soul is in God's hands. He said that anything, even a very small thing, should be considered and dealt with as a big one if it could cause dishonor or harm to our body or our assets.. Contrarily, something big that could not cause us major losses should be regarded as not really important. And this advice should be considered in everything we do and face in life. Coming back to our main subject:

If the wounds of one of my horses were not properly dressed —and the horse could die because of it —and if its bridle is broken because it was not properly checked by its caretaker, I should impose a reasonable punishment to the caretaker for not having properly dressed the horse's wounds (not only could the horse die but also it does not look good), and I should impose a very severe punishment for the broken bridle because it could put my life in jeopardy.

Chapter XVI—About the preparation of the stirrups and straps

It should be ensured that the stirrups are neither too wide nor too narrow; if they are too wide, the feet cannot stay firm and if they are too tight, the feet get hurt, we get tired much sooner and it is very dangerous as it would not be possible to take the feet out of them without difficulty. And the stirrup's soles should be neither too wide nor too narrow; if the soles are too wide we could not extend the feet; if the soles are too narrow they hurt the feet, we get tired easily, and in some situations we get cramps. The appropriate width for the stirrup's soles is, in my opinion, between two and two and a half fingers, if we are using French models. And the stirrups for Bravante saddles, even if others have different opinion, should be light in weight, small rather than big and not too wide; nevertheless, we should be able to put our feet in and out without difficulty. I invented a new model for the stirrups (for Bravante saddles and all the others): I ordered the stirrups with an appropriate casing around them.[20]

They are, in my opinion, and I already have great practice of them, very useful for foot protection and they also help us to ride stronger; and if we fall down, our feet are out of the stirrups more rapidly and they have other advantages to be found by those who decide to use them. The stirrup's straps should be as wide as possible (although they have to glide through the stirrup's eye),

---

[20] In leather? The author does not make any reference to the material the stirrup's casing is made of but it is for sure a material light in weight; this conclusion is due to the fact that the author has already said that the stirrup should be light in weight; it could be made of wood covered by leather.

strong, and should remain well fixed. And if we are riding a beast that gets wild, the straps should remain firmly in place; and I have seen some riders getting in serious trouble because they did not pay the due attention to the correct preparation of the stirrup's straps; it is very important they stay firmly in place. And I see that it is nowadays very common in Bravante saddles to place the stirrup's straps over the saddle flap, directly under your legs; it looks to be a good solution as they stay there in a safer way and are firmer.

Chapter XVII — About the preparation of the saddle

The saddle should be made of leather and the saddle-bows and all the other parts should be strong, resistant and firmly fixed, ensuring the stability and firmness of the whole set. And all should be prepared in such a way that the horseman could get the necessary help and support from the pommel and cantle.[21] The shape of the saddle's flap should have an adequate hollow for the horseman's [22]legs and the saddle's seat should be neither too long nor too short; on a long one, the horseman does not get the appropriate support from the seat and on a short one, he cannot hold himself correctly. And all should be checked to ensure that all is correct in accordance with the saddle's design. The main objective is to avoid parts that are imperfect or wrongly assembled and consequently, harm and injuries happen, as might be the case if the cantles are too straight, if

---

[21] The cantle is commonly divided in two parts; therefore, it is considered that there are two cantles and not only one. That's the reason why the author starts referring to "cantles" instead of "cantle."

[22] I use the words "horseman" and "rider" without any specific reason, just to avoid keying in the same word in every instance. The reader should consider them as synonyms.

[75]

the pommel is too high, if the saddle's flap does not have the adequate hollow for the horseman's legs, if the harness, the girth, the buckles or the stirrups are not in good condition or are wrongly assembled and as a result the whole arrangement is not as it should be and the horseman will be upset and troubled. And one should pay attention to the saddle's placement on the beast, because there are beasts which require the saddle to be placed more to the front or to the rear. And the horseman will get great help and advantage if everything is as it should be, principally if and when the beast misbehaves. If the beast usually bucks or kicks, we should place the saddle more to the front, nearer to the beast's shoulders. In a ship, the rolling is smaller if we are near the mast; for that reason, we should place the saddle more to the front, if the beast bucks or kicks. If the beast usually gets wild and rears, it is better to place the saddle more to its rear. For all these reasons I have ordered once again a new model of saddle with the cantles slightly curved and the hollows on the flap (for the horseman's legs) well marked; it resulted in greater advantages than we initially imagined, and it is very comfortable for long journeys.

Chapter XVIII — *About our own equipment*

When riding, we can get either help or embarrassment from the footwear, the spurs, the type of jerkin, the clothing, the sash and what we wear on the head.

The footwear should be tightened in the middle of the foot, thin at the toes, reasonably long, ample and not beaked at the end. If it is too thin and wide at the middle, it will hurt the foot and we will get tired quicker. And if it is short, rigid or too tight at the toes and beaked at the end, we can neither extend the foot nor make it firm in the stirrup. The spurs should have strong irons, rowels and straps;

all of them should be firmly fixed to the footwear. And if it is done that way, the horseman receives great help from the spurs. And their length should be in accordance with the type of saddle we are using and also with what we need to accomplish. Our footwear should be laced to be close-fitted; that way, we will feel ourselves calm and firm and not untidy. But we should avoid having the footwear too tight because that will cause us various difficulties. And if we are riding on a Gineta saddle, our footwear should be slightly more roomy and less strongly laced.[23]

The jerkin's design should be neither too tight—as we need to be able to move our body freely—nor too loose as it might become entangled somewhere, causing us difficulties; it should not stay loose on our body and if it is correctly tightened or laced, should be close-fitted at the neck. And if the jerkin's tail is long we should ensure that it is tight to our body in such a way that it does not go beyond the cantles on Bravante saddles. Even if this seems to be of no importance, I have seen some horsemen in great difficulties because of it.

The clothes should be reasonably short, in accordance with each one's habit, with sleeves that are light and not too big. I am sure that all horsemen feel themselves stronger if they wear light clothes instead of heavy ones which could cause difficulties to their movements. And if I have mentioned the clothes I can also address the armor; if the horsemen carry light armor, they can move faster in everything they have to do and therefore they will feel like stronger horsemen. There are some who say that that option is a disadvantage when they are not riding, but I say that being heavy in the saddle causes them to move slowly and it is much worse if they

---

[23] This is because your knees are bent and your heels are down. You need the room in your footwear to flex your ankle to achieve this leg/foot position.

get themselves unbalanced. Therefore the disadvantage is greater than the advantage. Nevertheless, I agree that heavier armor is advantageous for personal defense. And the clothing should be loose-fitting, for example a short mantle or the garment over the coat of mail, or others that are of the same type.

And those who wear sashes should wear them very tight around the waist. And if they feel embarrassed—due to the body they have—to wear the sash over their clothes, they could put it under them, very tight around the body, ensuring it does not slip down. On the head, we should not wear a big hood or a cowl but a small one or a hat with a large rim; if a horseman wears something heavy on his head, he could get in trouble if the beast misbehaves. And everything I have said, assumes that the beast you have mounted acts up frequently; in those situations everything, even the small things, could be very important. If that is not the case then there are certainly many other options available and everyone should wear what he considers best and more advantageous. The fact is that all those who think in advance about the difficulties that could arise, are better placed successfully to overcome them. And the best advice comes from one's own experiences. The choices should take advantage of the things that look to be better and more effective; because, on this subject—like in all the others— every man has his own preferences and his own solutions to overcome difficulties, which are not the same for all.

Chapter XIX — How and why some fall off the beast

I said before that we can fall off the beast forward, backward or to either side of the beast, as a consequence of any action we take, like handling and throwing a spear, striking with a sword, or any similar which we do not master as we should. It is a fact that most of the men who fall from the beast during a battle, a joust, a collision with an obstacle or due to a willful action from an opponent, are unable to avoid it due to lack of knowledge and will, and do not act as they should have; and most of them fall down because they could not get the proper help from their own bodies, legs, feet and hands. I am not saying all of them, because some suffer such violent collisions that it would have been impossible for them to stay mounted even if they were very strong. But if their will is strong and they know how to use their own advantages, they will be able — most of the time — to avoid falling down or suffering decisive collisions. And it happens that during a fight those who lack the will or required skills are unable successfully to face the enemy's strength or cunning, and fall down very rapidly.

And we have many examples of such situations in men's lives, as many fall down and start acting wickedly and living despicably, being unable to face as they should small setbacks and some difficult situations, due to failure of courage and knowledge of how to take good care of themselves and of their assets; and these situations will not happen to those who know how to overcome the difficulties they have to face, using their own qualities and the experience and advice from those who, having great knowledge and good experiences, give them the right counseling.

And it happens that those who are trying to act in difficult situations, sometimes fall to stratagems or tricks due to their weakness or greediness—both of them being a consequence of their lack of knowledge or ignorance; some are weak in character and when they need or want to do something become so confused that they fall down very rapidly. Coming back to our main subject: there are some who get so excited about doing specific actions (like handling and throwing a spear) that, due to impatience and ignorance, they forget how they should behave to stay mounted, and fall off the beast. I have seen a few falling down for exactly that reason: they grasp the spear so strongly that they are unable to handle it for a long time and when they are physically forced to let it fall down to the ground, they also go down, keeping it company; others throw the spear with so much energy that they get unbalanced and follow it out of the saddle! [24]Similar situations might happen when striking with a sword or doing any other thing; for lack of the necessary skills, many get unbalanced and fall down from the beast.

Chapter XX—How to fight using only the bare hands when mounted

There are riders who, either by necessity or just to play, fight against another rider, both unarmed and bare-handed, with the objective of throwing down the opponent.

---

[24] I laughed at those two points …is this D. Duarte's sense of humor?
There are two ways of striking with a spear (without throwing it): - Handling it in a horizontal position with the spear resting over the forearm;
-Handling it in non-horizontally (upwards or downwards) with its other end on the *axilla* (in the armpit).

The Art of Riding on Every Saddle

There are important recommendations that I am sure will be considered very useful by those who try them; and I am pleased to write about them.

First — Use one saddle with cantles that help you to stay firm (either supporting your lower back or enabling you to grasp one of them with one hand). And you should believe me when I say that it is preferable to use a Bravante saddle, even though it is not a great advantage; and of course, you must know how to keep yourself steady with the help of the cantle.

Second — Do not rely too much in staying firm in the stirrups, unless they are fixed to the horse's body; actually, if the stirrups are not fixed to the horse's body, they follow the movements of the rider's body and it is worse to be firm in them than the contrary.

Third — Try to unite yourself with the horse's body, sit firmly on the saddle and press your legs against the horse. Never relax the pressure of your legs when you grip your opponent; keep yourself steady and firm on the saddle's seat and grip your opponent in the best possible way.

Fourth — Grasp your opponent as high as possible or by one arm; it is easier to unbalance your opponent if you firmly grasp him by the upper part of his body or by one arm.

Fifth — If you see your opponent getting himself slightly unbalanced from the saddle to grasp you, take him by one arm and pull or push him sideways; as he is not properly seated on the saddle, it is easier to throw him off the horse.

Sixth — If you and your opponent are clinging to each other, you should try — as soon as possible — to force the hips of your opponent's horse to turn and simultaneously push or pull your opponent's body in any other direction. To better achieve this turning of the hips of your opponent's horse, you should keep your horse's head turned to the hips of your opponent's horse and never to the outside. Besides these points, everyone can find others that can be useful in specific situations. And if your objective is to throw your opponent's beast to the ground, there is one way that offers a good probability of success, if you know how to do it: you should firmly grasp the head of your opponent's beast by the bridle and push it upwards with a strong hand.

And all the ways referred above can be of great help to those who know them, if they are at ease on the horse and are strong horsemen; otherwise, they will not be able to do it.

Chapter XXI — How we should behave whenever we have to do all the things already described and other similar things

Independently of the things a horseman wants to do — and of his strong will to succeed — he should never forget that his main objective is — above everything — to stay firm and erect on the beast. As an example, whenever he is handling a spear, he should be more concerned with staying firm on the saddle and keeping his legs pressed against the beast's body rather than with the strength and resistance of his hand and arm to handle the spear. And when he is not able to keep the spear in his hand anymore, he should drop it, not attempting to do more than he can; because he must — above all — keep himself firm and safe on the saddle. And having this in mind, he should then use his hand, his arm and his body to correctly handle and throw the spear. And this is the way we should behave when we are mounted and want to do specific things, like striking with a spear or with a sword; we should never get ourselves unbalanced due to our body movements. And if we are used to acting this way, it would become natural. And this is a good advice, very useful and beautiful to those who know how to do it.

And we should consider this also useful to the various ways men live; some, not paying attention to the needs and obligations of their social positions and to the correct behavior they should consider for their lives, have such a strong desire to achieve a specific thing — even if it is worth almost nothing — that they fall down when they attempt to obtain what they are after. As a result, they have moments of great sadness and strong feelings of ill will and hate, even committing robberies and other similar acts, going after their desires without taking in consideration the real nature of what they are doing. But there are others who, even having the same strong desire of achieving a specific thing, would never attempt it without listening to their consciences and considering their social positions. And they surely are more successful in all their good deeds — and our Lord God would give them more credit — as it happens to those who have as the main objective of their lives to stay erect; and the riders who have the same objective — to stay erect and firm on the beast — are able to do everything much better than the others; and practicing these principles, they would acquire the experience they need to succeed in everything they do. And we should not value those who are not acting on the basis of these principles; and they would never be able to speak about them or to give good counsel; it is a fact that most men, although getting bad advice from others, go on with their lives in a proper way and will receive, when the due time comes, the appropriate reward. The good men do not feel forced to pay attention to all opinions, as they are very determined to always act with rectitude and honesty.

And those who, regardless of any immediate outcome, never change their strong will to act with rectitude and honesty, can expect to receive from our Lord God the reward that He always gratuitously gives to everyone, in accordance with their deeds.

This is the end of Section 1 (About being STRONG) and The beginning of Section 2 (About being FEARLESS)

Section 2 — About being FEARLESS

Chapter I - The many reasons men are fearless and how some men are fearless by nature

Having just finished the recommendations that horsemen stay strongly mounted, which is very important for the art of riding, I am now going to write about the recommendations to enable them to ride fearlessly, which is also an essential quality to all the good horsemen, especially if they are at war. And we should be aware that there are twelve[25] reasons why men — some more than others — are fearless in any specific action they take or situation they face, specifically: by nature, by presumption, by desire, by ignorance, by fortunate happenings, by custom, by reason, by fearing more another thing, by feeling themselves in advantage, by rage and by the grace of God.

First, some men are fearless by nature, because they were born that way and very rarely get ashamed or feel embarrassed, either in most of their actions or just in some specific ones. And there is one saying showing the value and strength of it: "What nature has given, no one can take away." And we see some being afraid of fights and not being afraid of the dangers of the seas; and others do not dare to fight or to face the dangers of the seas but are not afraid of plagues. And there are also those who feel so ashamed or embarrassed to do specific things publicly that they prefer to fall into very dangerous situations just to avoid others' criticism and

---

[25] Duarte lists eleven rather than twelve.

their consequent embarrassment. And there are others who would not have had any problem doing those things just because they are different by nature. About this, we should not forget that we can fail either by not daring enough or due to a total lack of fear, shame or embarrassment which can drive from acting in ways that are far beyond any reasonable limit. Therefore we can fail either by defect or by excess and we should not forget the saying: "Virtue is in the middle;" and we say about the effects of virtue's strength: it reduces fear and tempers the excess of boldness; but, in my opinion, it helps us to dare more rather than just avoid fear. And speaking about what we are by nature, I have the opinion that some are—by nature— fearless when they are riding or doing any other good thing; and this is in accordance with their good nature, because they desire and try to achieve only the things for which they are skilled. And to achieve them, they are reasonably bold; but at the same time, they fear the things they should and they run away from them in accordance with their reason. And I mention an example of these various attitudes: there are those who, by nature, dare too much and pass through fire and do other crazy things; there are others who are, by nature, cowards[26] and do not dare to do anything that looks to be even slightly dangerous; and finally, there are others who fear what they should and have the right level of courage to act as appropriate.

We have just discussed fear; now we are going to discuss shame and embarrassment.

---

[26] *Judeus* (Portuguese word for 'Jews') is the word the author wrote in the original text. The author could not hide his prejudice against Jews and considered they were all cowards. Unfortunately the author considered that "Jews" and "cowards" were synonyms; as translator I feel obliged to translate what the author wrote.

And I say that they are of different origins: **shame** is related to our *reason* and **embarrassment** is related to our *heart*. Reason makes us to feel ashamed whenever we attempt to do things we do not do well or things we believe we do not do well and could, therefore, be criticized by others. And we can feel too much or too little shame than we should or even not feel it at all in situations where we should. Really, we should feel shame in the same way as I said about boldness: in a balanced way. Embarrassment is totally related to our heart and consequently we do not know — most of the time — if it was caused by a good or bad thing. Many times, men feel embarrassed for certain things or situations in which they would have liked not to feel embarrassed. And this, in my opinion, is not advantageous unless it helps us to be afraid of becoming ashamed, preventing us to act in ways that could bring us real shame. In a word, embarrassment in itself is worth nothing. And everybody should try to avoid feeling embarrassed as much as possible, using his good sense and the habit, the practice and the strength of his will. And many men are mistaken when they listen to others who praise the fear of shame and they think that that is embarrassment and so they consider that embarrassment is a virtue; in reality, embarrassment is not a virtue and we should take it out of our heart as it limits and diminishes our will. We should not forget that shame's origin is the correct knowledge and evaluation of the situations and the errors committed so, if there is one thing that is an advantage — or even a virtue — it is shame and not embarrassment.

And I am not going to give more recommendations or additional teaching because the whole subject is about our nature, feelings whose consequences we cannot correct unless we have good reason and other things I have also mentioned. And when I decide to speak more about them I will write whatever I find appropriate. But I wrote this because I think it is necessary to understand what I am going to write later in this book and also because it is necessary that everyone should learn about his nature and about the reasons, feelings and emotions that are the driving force behind his acts. And although is commonly said that we cannot change our nature, I believe that men can reform themselves immensely, under God, correcting their shortcomings and increasing their virtues. And everyone should work hard to know himself better, maintaining and increasing the good virtues received and reducing his failures and correcting his shortcomings.

Chapter II — How presumption makes some men fearless

Due to their presumption of knowing how to do some specific things well, many men do them without fear and they say that — as they believe to know themselves — they have no doubts about which things they know well; and being sure about which things they know well, they do them with less fear than the things they presume not to do that well. Nevertheless, many times it happens that we are more afraid of doing something we normally do well than other things we cannot do so well; and this happens due to same of the twelve[27] reasons already referred and it is a fact that the presumption of knowing how to do something well might not be sufficient to do it fearless as it is possible that other reasons cause some fear. But under normal circumstances it is true that knowing — or having the presumption — to do something well enables us to do it fearlessly.

In riding, like in all the things we want to do, if fear makes us unable to do it well we should, first of all, learn how to do it better; and if we know how to do it well, we will have the aforementioned

---

[27] Recall that Duarte illustrates eleven, rather than twelve.

presumption which in itself normally causes most or all the fear to vanish.

Chapter III — How desire makes some men fearless

As we all know some men, due to the desire they feel, are not afraid of doing certain things. It is said that fear is not very important as a factor for those who have a strong desire about a specific thing; if the desire is sufficiently strong, men will overcome the fear they might feel. As this is common knowledge it is not necessary to write more about it. But, to go on as I have started, I write about what I have learned; everything we do freely — as a consequence of our will — is to achieve one of these four objectives: recreation, profit, honor and honesty. And it is said that when we do something just to satisfy our sense of honesty or when we do it just for the love of any specific virtue, we do not have any intention of gaining additional profit, recreation or pleasure as it is enough for us to know that we are doing what we should, without looking for any other recompense or reward. And we can illustrate this attitude in the following way: If a lord gives a special grace to his people, doing what he considers his moral obligation without having any intention of gaining a profit, he will know that due to his attitude and decision he would be better loved and served; nevertheless, his main motivation — which touches and warms his heart — is to feel he is fulfilling his desire to do good. And whenever some thing is done just because of this desire, it is considered that it is done with an honest objective. And all desires are motivated by one of these four situations: a good intention, a bad intention, the objective of gaining profit (which in itself is not a sin) or just because we want to do it. Whatever the motivation or the situation, I am sure that a strong desire helps to be fearless in everything we have to do. And if due to the expectations of profit, sailors are not afraid to face the dangers of the seas and thieves do not fear justice, nobody should doubt that if someone desires to become a good horseman, his will would be sufficient to enable him to overcome the fear of falling from the horse— or with it—and therefore he will end up being a good horseman.

Chapter IV—How ignorance makes some men fearless

There are those who, due to ignorance, are fearless. There is a saying covering this situation, "Experienced birds are afraid of the lasso." And the ignorance comes from two sources: the reason or the heart.

From the reason, we are aware of extant dangers, because our mind keeps what we have seen and heard and their consequences; so, we are afraid of the harm we can face and suffer. And we can also be afraid, knowing of some specific situation in the past and assuming that the same outcome can also happen to us, even if the situation we are facing is not similar. And this kind of fear is always justified and our reason orders us to do what is good and be afraid of the contrary. And if we are afraid of situations we should not be, it is not due to our reason that we are unable to identify what is good or do not want to do what is right, but to our ignorance. And there are some who do not understand the situation they have to face, and are brave, and there are others who are prudent and have too much fear; but I say that those who without understanding a situation are brave, do not show any specific virtue; for that to be true they would have had to face the situation being aware of its risks and dangers and having made the decision because they were driven by the satisfaction and pleasure of doing good deeds. And this is true to everything that is virtuous; and we can feel the satisfaction and pleasure of having faced and overcome the dangers only after we have achieved our objectives and never during the course of the action. And if someone is afraid and acts with too much prudence and caution, that might happen for two reasons: due to fear, he does not know what he should do or, knowing it, his heart chooses — due to lack of strength and fear — the wrong course of action.

In regard to reason it is important for us to know what is dangerous and what it is not — even if it looks to be — in the art of riding; and we should be afraid of the really dangerous actions and situations and not be afraid of all the others. Because, relative to all situations, knowing them enables us to be afraid of the really dangerous ones and not be afraid of all the others — even if they look to be dangerous. In regard to the heart: the heart knows the dangers of some situations it has already faced, either over time or at a certain moment when it faced a specific situation. And it might not feel afraid but it might feel conflicting sentiments in such a way that it could be afraid of things that it was not formerly afraid of. And a person might not feel afraid after he had won a fight during which he was hurt; this is due to the fact that the success of the fight overcame the fear in his heart. In a word, we can decide to do dangerous things but only ignorance can produce a total absence of fear; and we should protect ourselves from our heart's feelings and act always based on our reason.

We should be aware of the various dangers involving the art of riding, avoiding painful learning experiences to our heart; if those situations happen, our heart might become so frightened that we might never be able to control our heart's fear. And those who have the knowledge and are aware of the existing dangers, either because they know them by experience or because they were taught will be, under God, protected from disasters; and in the things they decide to do based on their reason, they will have the appropriate audacity in some situations and fear and prudence in others.

Chapter V—How fortunate occurrences make some men fearless; how youngsters and others who are starting learning the art of riding should be taught

It is well known that fortunate occurrences make men fearless and I do not need to write more about it because it is clearly proven by experience. Nevertheless I should note that it is said by some that good meat dishes and other kinds of good food also make men fearless. One of the fortunate occurrences that helps the correct learning of the art of riding is to have from the start good and appropriate beasts, in accordance with each one's stage of learning; because the beasts should be of one type at the beginning and of other types later on.

As it is now the proper time to approach this subject, it should be noted that a youngster or any other person who is starting to learn the art of riding should do it initially on a healthy beast with no signs of malice or evil intentions; bridle, girth, stirrups, and saddle, should be of good quality and it should be ensured that the beast is well-harnessed. So, it is of the utmost importance that he gets a beast he can easily mount feeling himself safe, regardless of his initial ability or aptitude. And if he starts making mistakes we should not reprimand him severely, but gently and little by little. And we should praise him with enthusiasm whenever he acts correctly and starts showing gradual development. And we should act this way until we see he has really decided to go on learning and is actually looking forward to being corrected and taught.

From that moment onwards we should start teaching him everything necessary to enable him to stay strongly mounted, because this is the most important of all the various skills he would need; and we should go on flattering him whenever there is a reason for it and—of course— correcting him always in the nicest possible way. And if he falls down from the horse, if his feet come out of the stirrups or if he does any other thing that is contrary to the art of riding, we should show we understand and excuse him in the nicest possible way letting him know that he should not lose the will to go on learning and the hope of becoming a good horseman. This methodology of teaching is very important not only for this learning process but also for many other things in life. And we should convince him to have the good habit of riding frequently which is much better than riding for a long time but only once in a while. And when he starts galloping and jumping he should start cantering and jumping over easy obstacles like wooden bars or thick sticks left on the ground. And when he starts jumping over them we should teach him how to do it correctly. And he should go on mounting the same beast until he looses all fear. When we see that he can gallop and jump over easy obstacles fearlessly, it is the appropriate time to start choosing more difficult obstacles for him to jump over and beasts more difficult to control, to get him used to some additional difficulties like beasts that kick, hop and do other evil things with malice. And we should not allow him to get back to docile and sweet-tempered beasts because his will could be weakened and he could become lazy if he gets back to the easy situations he got when he started learning the art of riding, thus not gaining awareness and preparation for the difficulties he is going to face in real life. And he should learn to be strongly mounted on every type of saddle, to go over difficult ground—up and down hill—and to learn how to maneuver and throw a spear; and he should start learning the maneuvering of a spear using a lightweight one, because it is easier to learn the correct arm and body movements that way. And when they start learning how to maneuver a spear we should choose one without sharp ends to avoid any disaster; they can use pointless canes or wooden sticks with a weight in accordance with their strength enabling them to learn the art of maneuvering and throwing a spear without danger.

After a student is skilled and able to control any beast—even the most difficult—it is the time to choose good horses for him, with the appropriate harnesses. And coming to the last stages of the learning process it is the time for him to be severely reprimanded for every error done and force him to repeat his movements and actions as many times as necessary until correction and perfection are ensured and obtained. And from time to time he should get back to the difficult beasts, enabling him not to forget what he should do in difficult situations. And he should also practice riding without stirrups and other difficult situations that might happen in real life, ensuring he is prepared for them, if and when they happen. Nevertheless, he should not be put in situations of real danger.

And all those who are lucky enough to have good teachers—a most fortunate happening—have a unique opportunity of becoming fearless horse riders.

There are additional specific needs to ride in jousts, tournaments and in war. Most of them could and should be practiced and learned properly; that way, we will be prepared—under God—to use our knowledge and power whenever we find ourselves in those difficult and dangerous situations. And if we do that, we should be able to behave in the best possible way at all times.

Chapter VI—How by habit some men are fearless

Habit reduces men's fear of doing certain things, if there are no other reasons to maintain their fear. Nevertheless, it is said that doing things a man is used to does not arouse the emotions.

About the consequences of habit: we should be aware that if we do not maintain the habit of riding wild and restless beasts, galloping and jumping over moderately dangerous grounds and obstacles, our will becomes weaker and fear, embarrassment and shame could influence us in such a way that the important ability we had could be greatly reduced or even totally lost.

Therefore, those who want to remain strong riders should never lose the habit (for any reason like for example, age or laziness) of, once in a while, riding wild beasts to avoid having their hearts conquered by fear. If they do not maintain that habit, fear will increase and they will not be able to remain good riders.

Chapter VII — How due to reason men are fearless

Some men do not fear to do a specific thing because their reason tells them that they should not be afraid of it. That is why it is said that animal's acts are ruled by nature and instinct whereas men make decisions in accordance with their reason. But this does not happen to all because there are weak men ruled only by nature and strong men ruled by the strength of their reasoning power. And there is one main difference between them: there are men who know so little that they are unable to differentiate between good and evil or have such a strong will that it blinds their reason; others, being good men, decide their acts always in accordance with their reason and as such, many force themselves to do things they really dislike or not to do things they would like to only because their reason advises them that way and they do not act against it; this happens with well-bred youngsters who do not act without prior approval from their mentors, guides or counselors.

And those who act this way will not lose the habit and the courage to do the things their reason tells them not to be afraid of, even if they really feel some fear due to any other cause. It is therefore vital that knights and squires are really aware of the importance for their lives of the art of riding and so are not afraid of learning it and practicing it frequently. In order to achieve the benefits of being good riders and to avoid the difficulties of those who do not have those skills, they should exert their will and maintain the habit of riding, enabling them not to forget that ability with age; because it is a well known fact that most men are afraid of galloping and jumping when riding wild beasts. And if their reason does not force them to keep that habit they will lose it completely. And if they allow that to happen, their fear will increase and their ability to ride will deteriorate, as has already been said. But knowing the consequences of losing the habit of riding frequently, everyone should listen to their reason and keep the will necessary to ride, maintaining the level of daring that only habit could provide. And we should be aware that, though youngsters do not fear falls too much, men do; actually, fear increases along with the rider's age. Therefore, as we should advise the youngsters to be moderately afraid of riding through some kinds of dangerous grounds, we should also advise the not so young to keep the habit of riding frequently in order to avoid being influenced by cowardice.

Chapter VIII — How by feeling themselves at an advantage or by fearing another thing more, men become fearless

Some men, knowing they have advantages over others, are fearless doing certain specific things; this happens in many situations such as the use of force, the art of riding, the knowledge of other important arts and the use of weapons; and all these situations happen in accordance with each one's knowledge of himself and of his opponent's skills. Therefore, it is most advantageous for each one of us to learn as many important arts as possible. And in order to be a fearless rider it is very important to have good and well-harnessed beasts; under these conditions it is easier to dare whenever necessary whereas if the conditions are not that favorable there are reasons for fear to install itself in one's heart.

It is a well known fact that men are less afraid of doing a certain thing if they are also facing another thing they fear more. For example, some men in ship at the dock jump ashore, breaking some bones because they have more fear of the sea; others, throw themselves from the roof of their homes because they are more afraid of an on-going fire. That's why it is said that a strong emotion overcomes a weaker one. Knights and squires who are afraid of learning how to ride can get help from the knowledge that it is even more dangerous for them if they do not know it; out of this knowledge, they will gain a strong determination to overcome the fear and embarrassment they feel starting to learn the art of riding — and of falling from the horse or with it — enabling them to become — in due time — good horsemen.

Chapter IX — How due to rage some men become fearless

It is well known how due to the rage they feel many men completely lose the fear they normally have of certain things. There is a discussion about rage: is it a good thing or a bad thing? Having in consideration all the arguments in favor and against, my position is as follows: Rage is not a desirable feeling for good men because their strong will and understanding, self-control and strength are what they need to live their lives correctly. There is only one situation in which rage could be useful for such men, helping them to correct their behavior: if they feel rage against themselves either for having done something wrong or for having felt rage against someone without a proper reason.

Although rage could be useful for weak-hearted and submissive men, nevertheless, it must not be too intense as it might cause them to act blindly without any kind of self-control. Therefore, rage could be useful only if it enables them to act in accordance with their good reason in situations where they do not have—under normal circumstances—the necessary strength and determination to do what should be done. Coming back to my main point: if, when riding, knights and squires do anything wrong due to their ignorance and because of it feel rage against themselves, normal good reason would force them to work hard and learn what they need without fear or embarrassment, which they would have been unable to do otherwise if they did not feel rage against themselves.

So, under these aforementioned circumstances—and only under these —rage could be a useful feeling as it helps men to control or get rid of the fear and do specific things they should and need to do.

Chapter X—How by the grace of God some men become fearless

Despite it being well-known that to be skilled in an important art or to have a specific virtue it is necessary to deserve a special grace from our Lord God, I put forward the following:

• If a man, who is normally more afraid than he should, faces a really dangerous situation fearlessly and acts with great honor, how could it be explained unless through a special grace conceded to him by God?

• If men who are fearless in everything they do, fail and dishonor themselves in a specific situation, isn't it the consequence of having been abandoned by God due to their sins? This being said — and kept in mind — we should always act to deserve the grace of God, which is essential to enable us not to lose the ability of riding and all the other important things we do well due to the virtues conceded by Him.

I have already written many times and at length about this because I know many men who, having much more fear than they should of learning the art of riding — and to do other important things — do not have, as a consequence, the skills which would represent for them great advantages and additional honors.

And if each one knows the various reasons why he might feel fear, it is possible — under God — to find the required strength to learn how to overcome fear, always acting in accordance with good reason, correcting his errors and reducing his shortcomings; in a word — overcoming at its origin the evil which is the cause for the inhibition to act properly.

This is the end of Section 2 — About being Fearless And the beginning of Section 3 — About Safety

Section 3—About Safety

Chapter I - How to obtain safety

A man who is not afraid of riding has the capability to stay strongly mounted, maintaining a posture that reflects his strong will and simultaneously shows off how safe he feels. Nevertheless there are those who—for some reasons I have already referred to—are not afraid of riding but are unable to show their strong will and how safe they feel. As an example, let us consider a melancholic person who has decided to do something stupid about which his heart still feels some fear, shame or embarrassment; even if he does that thing, overcoming the fear he feels, he would not be able to show off— through a correct posture—the strong will and safety that are characteristics of every good horsemen.

Above all the other things that—as I already said—makes a man fearless when doing a specific thing, there are four who are the most important ones, namely: nature, presumption, habit and reason. And as I have also already said how nature, presumption and habit make fear disappear and allow safety to be obtained, I still have to declare how reason ensures, maintains and enables us to demonstrate safety.

Actually we should take into consideration that, as a strong will usually produces safety, we have to avoid or overcome the five main reasons which diminish our will, namely: being afraid of doing a specific thing; doing it hastily; doing it too late or lazily; feeling ourselves embarrassed when doing it; doing it with more care than we should.

[100]

Chapter II — How both fear and haste show lack of safety

To better explain this statement I am going to use an example: If a man, when riding, is afraid of the danger or ashamed of a specific situation it is a fact that — in that situation — his will is not strong and he no longer feels safe. This is because fear and safety both belong to his heart but they cannot reside there simultaneously. Therefore, if a man is afraid of something, he cannot feel himself safe. And if due to rage or any other of the reasons already mentioned, he dares to ride a beast that becomes wild or he decides to do something that is not safe, others who know him well would recognize that from his face, his attitude and posture of his body.

It is well known that acting hastily most certainly means lack of safety; if you — by any reason — are afraid of doing a specific thing, it is only natural that you would try to finish it as quickly as possible; so, it is a well known sign that you are not doing one specific thing with the appropriate level of safety if you are doing it hastily. But you can act in a specific situation rapidly and zealously (and therefore without unnecessary delays) and this is a totally different situation, because there is a major difference between the two circumstances.

To do one thing vigorously and zealously avoids unnecessary delays and shows safety; whereas if you act hastily, it means you have fear in your heart and in most situations you do whatever you are doing badly and with a lack of safety.

Chapter III — How perturbation, embarrassment and acting slowly and late show a lack of safety.[28]

All the feelings and sentiments we have in our hearts are known only to ourselves, whereas everybody knows and evaluates us only by our acts; therefore it is only natural that, if someone takes more time than it is considered normal to do a certain thing, many could think and say that he is not sure and does not feel sure about what he is doing. Nevertheless, if someone does a specific thing quickly just because it is his nature or if he does it slowly and lazily also because it is his nature, it might be considered that he is acting in that way due to fear, shame or embarrassment when, in reality, it is just due to his nature.[29]

---

[28] In the first three chapters of this Section 3 the author deals with external signs of one's behavior and attitude or posture which could be taken as reflecting lack of safety. It is my understanding that the author's aim was to warn the readers to be aware that, in reality, they might be mistaken by the external signs and that, therefore, they must be careful in the interpretation of the real causes for one's behavior's external signs. The author rarely says, "...*there is a lack of safety*..." but instead he prefers to say, "...*it shows lack of safety*...." The author's final message (Chapter III) is that we have to know well a person to understand the real level of safety of his acts.

[29] I am very impressed with the author. What percentage of D. Duarte's XV century readers really understood some of his messages? And what about the readers of the XXI century?

Chapter IV—How being too careful shows lack of safety

As we know, being afraid of something and fear itself are obstacles to safety. When someone is more careful than he should be when doing a specific thing that is normally a proof that his heart does not feel safe; because if you are afraid of some eventual danger when doing a specific thing it is only human to be too diligent in order to have it finished as soon as possible. And everyone who sees you acting that way easily understands that you do not feel safe; actually, when you are afraid of something or feeling fear itself in your heart when you are doing a specific thing, that situation is normally understood by many, before, during and after you are doing that specific thing. And I give examples of it: If someone is challenged to ride a wild horse and he refuses because he is afraid and he does not have the courage to do it, he clearly shows that he does not have a strong will. And if he, nevertheless, begins his preparations to ride the wild beast, it is almost sure that he either takes longer than he should or acts hastily. Both situations show lack of safety; this type of situation also happens if it is only required to gallop normally and to make reasonable jumps and even so the rider takes a long time in his preparation; most probably, he will be so rigid and stiff on the beast that it is clear to everybody that he feels unsafe. In a word—whenever someone shows being more diligent than necessary when doing a specific thing, it is a clear sign that he feels unsafe.

Chapter V—How we can act safely and show it off

Everything we have written so far has had the objective of showing how safety can fail us; therefore, we should learn as well as possible how we can get, maintain and show it, because if we are able to protect ourselves from everything that threatens our safety we achieve everything we need to act safely. And I put forward one example: if a person feels himself unsafe when riding, due to the fear, shame or embarrassment he feels, he should take in consideration everything I wrote about what is necessary not to be afraid and act accordingly; I believe that, if he does as I said, he will achieve the security he needs to ride normally. And besides all these, if he rides only good beasts, he will certainly greatly improve his riding I also wrote about perturbation, embarrassment, haste and acting with too much diligence or care; everyone should consider whether he might fail due to anyone of these things because, if he does not know his limitations and the reasons behind them, he will not have the possibility to correct and overcome them. If he knows he failed in one situation due to haste, he should start acting in similar situations with deliberate slowness until he considers he has overcome his limitations. And if there are other reasons for his failures he should carefully choose to act in an opposite way until his limitations are corrected. This advice is only based in common sense: if you want to straighten a wooden stick or a curved cane you have to apply the appropriate strength from the opposite direction. You should act similarly concerning the limitations you want to get rid of and the virtues you are after.

In a word—we should deliberately act with excessive determination until our heart tells us that we can get back to our normal behavior because our objectives were achieved.

[104]

And if, when riding, our heart feels too safe and we do not feel the need to keep the required alertness, our reason should intervene to ensure that we do not act negligently but with the required care.

At the other extreme, if we feel we should act with great or even too much care to protect ourselves from a specific danger that might occur, out heart should prevent that, telling us that we could be censured by others if we act that way.

Between these two antagonistic attitudes, each one of us should make his own decision and our reason should decide how we should act, because most of the time, we do not act in total accordance with our heart.

And many times in life we face a dilemma: on one hand, we should act always in accordance with our reason so nothing should be left to chance, and on the other, we should also be aware how little is our knowledge and power and that—despite all the measures we can take to protect ourselves—we are under our Lord God. So, we should always act with moderation and we should not hesitate to do whatever is appropriate to our situation, age and mood, taking in consideration what is done by those we respect and regard highly, and above all not forgetting that our main responsibility to ourselves is to stay prepared for the countless dangers that we surely are to face throughout our life.

And without losing the habit of using our reason, we should protect ourselves from everything we possibly can—which we would not be able to do without the help of our Lord God; and, if and when necessary, we should do everything that is required from us, even if danger is visible.

With all these examples I hope to have made clear how men of good understanding could achieve the maximum possible safety during their actions and simultaneously showing it off. This becomes possible due to the knowledge they have of their own limitations and shortcomings and the efforts they make to correct themselves, acting always in the most appropriate manner in everything they do.

Chapter VI — How one's attitude can show safety

It is possible to show off our safety when we are doing specific things, faking it through the use of specific attitudes that normally reflect safety. That ability is not only useful to deceive others; if we do it frequently, these activities might become a habit and eventually convince our heart; we could end up really feeling safe! Here are some examples:

• When riding a wild beast or if you want to do something and you are not sure about the beast's reaction, you should always show a pleasant and quiet attitude; nevertheless, you should not exaggerate or overstate it as your attitude might be taken by others as fake and your level of safety would be considered even lower than it really is.

• If the beast prances, bucks, kicks or goes in circles, you should use one of your hands and — slowly and calmly — set in order your hood or any other specific piece of clothing, looking like a rider who is not worried at all with anything the beast could do because you are strongly mounted and feeling absolutely safe; nevertheless, you should neither do these type of actions too frequently nor always use the same gestures; and you should also not spend more time doing those actions than the time considered normal to do them.

• If you need to press your legs tightly against the beast's belly, to use the spurs frequently or to pull the bridle or the reins to control the beast, you could at sometime go on talking to your companion about any subject, showing that you are not in any trouble; and you should keep the same attitude and posture talking and listening to others during the period of time you need to control the beast. Acting this way you are showing that even riding a fierce beast you feel so safe and strongly mounted, that you can pay attention to the ongoing conversation. If your companion is on foot you should lean your upper body slightly in his direction, showing you are not afraid of falling down; and as everybody is paying attention, you should also look directly at them, even if the beast gets really wild. So, there is one general rule to keep in mind: Whatever action the beast does, either on its own initiative or by our command, we should always show ourselves strongly mounted, comfortable and having fun, as if we were just riding leisurely and not at all embarrassed.

There are many more examples we could describe, but those who are reading these pages can easily find others equally useful from their own experience.

In summary—If you master perfectly these various attitudes you can do them in such a way that you are able to show off that you are really safe and not faking it.

Chapter VII—Doubts about one's attitudes which concern giving the impression of safety

Some say that the attitudes described in the previous chapter should not be done by good men because they should never use methods which are not really truthful. On the contrary, their acts should be always clean and pure; and, using these types of deceptions, the good men could get used to lying in other situations; once they get used to doing it in the situations described in the last chapter they could do it in other unjustified and indefensible situations.

To these considerations I say that this showing off and deception are done with good intentions, as good men want their hearts used to overcoming difficult situations which happen when they are riding wild beasts and they are not causing any damage to anybody; so, I do not consider these attitudes I have just described as a sin and, in my opinion, they can be done without causing embarrassment or criticism to one's conscience. And I am sure that good men will not get used to lying in other circumstances, which cause him to commit a sin or to get censured.[30]

This is the end of Section 3 - About Safety And the beginning of Section 4 - About Quietness

---

[30] In my opinion, the author's justification for one's behavior in this chapter VII it is not very easy to accept. I think they do not match the author's previous discussion of ethics. It looks he accepts —at the least— white lies.

Section 4 — About QUIETNESS[31]

Chapter I - How a skilled horseman should match his body quietness with the beast's behavior

Having written about three things:

1. About being *strong*, which is the most important of everything for a horseman

2. About being *fearless* and audacious

3. About *safety*, which is very important for riding and many other things I am going now to write—in less detail—about the tranquility of the horseman and the quietness of his body. And, in order to have the appropriate level of quietness on the saddle it is of the utmost importance to be strongly mounted, fearless and to feel safe; and I am going to spend some time describing how all these should be accomplished. Some think that tranquility and body quietness show lack of agility but that is not so; on the contrary, tranquility is a great help to agility, as it will be described later.

---

[31] About the translation of the word *assessego*. This word is frequently used in this Section Four and in so many different situations that if sometimes it should be translated by quiet/quietness of the whole body (or parts of it); there are other situations in which we have to use the word "tranquility" (which in my opinion expresses better the author's idea that the word "calm"). In summary—we can consider the quietness of the body as a physical consequence of the tranquility the horseman feels; the author clearly interconnects them; but we have to use either one or the other, in accordance with the context.

A good horseman is able to match his level of tranquility with the beast's behavior; for an example, if he is just riding leisurely, his body should not be too quiet and rigid, his legs should not be extended to their limit and his upper body should not be too firm and stiff as all these would show that he is embarrassed or is afraid of the beast. He should instead show a natural agility in his entire body as if he were walking.

Nevertheless, he should not show carelessness on the saddle—as it always looks bad—but on the contrary he should show a firm attitude and a level of body quietness appropriate to the type of saddle; if he acts as he should, the attitude of his body will show the natural agility he has and simultaneously that he is a fearless and unembarrassed horseman.

In general, the horseman's tranquility and his body quietness should be in accordance with the beast he is mounting and the type of ground he is traveling across. And if the beast is trotting or galloping, it looks good to show more firmness and quietness of the body; and if the beast then gets wild, the horseman should clearly show firmness on his attitude, quietness of his body and security in the saddle.

Chapter II—How should body quietness and tranquility should be obtained, kept and shown

Body quietness applies mainly to the upper body, above the knees (because they should never reduce their pressing on the beast's body). Our feet should be firm in the stirrups, as I always do; I wrote about it when I described the various styles of riding required by the types of saddles used. If the beast starts galloping with no previous warning or gets wild, our face should show no traces of embarrassment and our head should not move around unnecessarily; nevertheless, whenever we find it appropriate to move or want to look at something specific we should move our face the same way we do when we are walking around. We should keep our shoulders tight, our body erect or slightly leaning to anyone of the sides, not because we need it to control the beast but to show that we are really at ease and therefore we have body positions simultaneously safe and harmonious. If we are maneuvering or throwing a spear or doing any other thing, we should keep our upper body quiet and firm ensuring that — whatever the beast tries to do — we can always stay in control using the spurs and the hands (for the spear or the reins), showing no signs of embarrassment and an attitude as quiet as if we were riding leisurely or just walking around.

To ensure tranquility all over our body we should — above everything — have our feet quiet and firm in the stirrups, and it is of the utmost importance that the stirrup straps have the same length. If we have the habit of riding with our feet totally inside the stirrups, the stirrup straps should have an adequate length to enable our heels to stay reasonably low; and we should not bend our feet (as if they were our legs) trying to hold them on to the horse's belly.[32]

If we have the habit of holding our feet in the stirrups by their middles, our heels should be kept a bit lower with our insteps always tense because most of the body quietness and tranquility comes from there.[33]

---

[32] In other words, we should not use our heels and a cramped calf to grasp at the horse's side, which would make the heels come up and the toes point downwards, thus "bending the feet."

[33] The reason why this causes tranquility and quietness in your body is because when riding, you must allow your joints to be shock absorbers,

Our last word on this subject—horsemen should take always great care in the preparation of the saddle and the stirrups as they are of great importance to enable their overall safety.

Chapter III—About body quietness, tranquility and their advantages

The tightening of the shoulders and the stiffening of their bodies make horsemen gallop firmly, harmoniously and beautifully.

And they should be ready to set the spurs to his horse whenever necessary; from the knees down, the legs should remain quiet unless there is the need to set the spurs on the beast. No horseman should keep his arms tight to his body because if he needs to move them he loses the quietness of his upper body; so, whenever there is a need to maneuver the reins or any other thing that makes the horseman to move his arms, he should always maintain his body quiet, firm and erect; and he should get help from his hands, arms and feet whenever he feels that need but he should not move his body more than is strictly necessary.

A good horseman should keep his body quiet and firm and the weapons he carries should not be moving around as it is very prejudicial to the agility the horseman needs and it does not look good; and the horsemen who are more firm on the saddles are the who are able to keep their weapons still.

---

and with the toe lifted, your ankle becomes flexed and becomes more of a shock absorber than if your toes are pointed downward and your ankle locked.

The tranquility of a horseman, when mounted, receives great help from him being vigorous, at ease and harmonious and carrying within his hands reach most of the things he might need to handle. And those who really want to become good horsemen need to work hard until they are able to show quietness of body, face and attitude; and in order to achieve all these they should learn through the examples given by those who are considered to be the best in the art of riding.

This is the end of Section 4 — About quietness And the beginning of Section 5 — About being at ease

Section 5 — About being at EASE

Chapter I - About being at ease and having a free and strong will

As it is written in the introduction of the THIRD PART its now the time to approach the subject of being at ease when mounted. A rider who is at ease when mounted on the beast shows he has none of the limitations that exist in many cases and that are mainly due to embarrassment, weakness of the will, shame, lack of physical ability, ignorance of the art of riding and lack of practice. And I believe it is necessary to take care of them in order to be able to show how we can get rid of those limitations, and so acquiring the easiness, the fluency of movement and the self-confidence we all need whenever we ride.

Most of the aforementioned limitations are directly related to our will and many riders feel constrained by embarrassment, weakness and shame.

I have already covered this subject and explained how this situation could be — up to a certain point — overcome; but, in order to reinforce it, I feel appropriate to mention some books I have read in which it is described one important human virtue — greatness of heart. It is written that a man with that virtue has the right self-esteem and self-confidence necessary for always acting the way all good men could and should act.

And that statement should be true: nevertheless, if someone has a good opinion about himself and is worth much less, he is presumptuous; and, if he is really able to do the things much better than he thinks he is, then it is said he has a small or weak heart. It is then required from those who have this virtue (greatness of the heart) to have the right level of self-esteem and self-confidence to always perform—good and great deeds—in accordance with their real capabilities. The Philosopher[34] said that he was very doubtful about the possibility of anyone to know the exact measure of his own value; that being true, anyone with greatness of the heart would most probably presume for himself a value a little bigger than the reality and not the contrary. And those with this virtue—greatness of heart—would always perform with great ease, if that virtue is great enough to cover all their actions; and it also happens that those who think that they probably would not be able to do a specific thing correctly would have their will very much weakened when attempting to succeed. But those who expect to succeed do not feel constrained by the possibility of an initial failure because they would understand how to quickly correct themselves in order to succeed; so, they will always attempt to do everything they consider they should or want to do. This is in general terms, because there are some who feel this virtue only for certain things; that's the reason why there are those who feel no problems in riding but are unable to dance; others feel at ease when in combat but are unable to sing; and similar examples happen in many other situations. But—and as a conclusion —those who have that virtue—greatness of heart—covering what they are doing, are much more at ease when attempting to succeed.

Relative to shame, some are very restrained for lack of good understanding, practice, conversation or advice. I consider appropriate to repeat what I said before about the difference between shame and embarrassment.

---

[34] Aristotle

Embarrassment comes from the heart and as such, influences negatively everything, even the good things that should be done. Shame comes from the reason and as such, influences negatively any specific thing which is considered by a person as not proper to be done; so, the person stops its practice and becomes embarrassed if required to do it, not being at ease as it would be in normal circumstances. Even if the decision taken of not doing that specific thing is proven to be wrong, that error comes from the reason and shame is the cause of the embarrassment felt. Those who want to feel at ease doing a specific thing, need to get rid of the embarrassment and that could be achieved through practice and the presumption in their own capabilities; seeing that others—who are not better than they—are able to do it, they should presume that they could do it at least as well as the others do; this way—as an example—anyone should assume that he would be able to perform as well as any other of his fellow creatures when riding. And we should not consider that, due to presumption, one should be disdainful or vain; even if we feel inclined to be disdainful or vain— if we are good and virtuous men—we should always be polite and to deal honorably with everybody. Relative to reason, it is most important to have a good understanding about the capabilities that we need to use, in accordance with our age, status, situation and circumstances. And those things that need to be done must be done. Even if our heart tries to convince us not to act, we should force it to lose the embarrassment, the shame and the laziness through frequent practice, as this is the way to feel at ease, which is required for everything we want to do properly.

Chapter II—About physical ability, knowledge and skills of specific activities—namely riding—and how best to achieve them

There are some who are knowledgeable and skilled in the art of riding or in other activities and there are even those who have great advantage in everything they do, or in just some of the things they do. Actually, the physical ability for a specific activity is not determined just by having the appropriate constitution as there are some who look, at first sight, as not having the minimum body characteristics suitable for the practice of some activity or activities and it turns out that they do them with great ease; and the contrary also happens to others.

It is my belief that our Lord God gave to some who have a strong will to be skilled in a specific art the necessary daring and perseverance they need not to despair, even if their body does not look to be the most appropriate for the practice of that specific art or activity; and they are able to persevere seeing others with similar physical characteristics practicing the art or activity they sought with great ease. In my opinion, there are more who are unable to be knowledgeable and skilled in a specific art or activity due to their lack of a strong will than the ones who cannot achieve it just due to their physical limitations; nevertheless, I concede that there are some who, by nature, do excel in riding whereas there are others so limited physically that only through a lot of hard work are able to feel at ease when mounted on a beast. But, besides all these things related to nature, there are four main factors only related to the teachings aspects of riding which concern the ability to be at ease when mounted on a beast:

1. How to use and move the right arm to maneuver and throw a spear, to strike with a sword or to perform any other thing.[35]

2. How to use and move the left hand and arm to hold and control the reins as necessary.

3. How to position and keep the legs and the knees when mounted and how and when to use the spurs.

4. How to have the proper attitude and countenance of the face and the body as described by me in the chapter about safety.

And to be at ease when riding we should not have our arms and legs rigid and tightly connected to the body; on the contrary, they should be able to move freely and at ease, doing whichever action they need to perform in every moment and situation, whereas the body stays quiet.

Actually, this is one of the main aspects that identify a good horseman; those who are able to keep their bodies quiet achieve, more easily than others, the objective of becoming good horsemen.

---

[35] It is interesting to note that throughout all his book, D. Duarte never really considers the possibility of a person to be left-handed; all his teachings and descriptions assume that everybody is right-handed . Only once does he refer to the possibility of doing a specific action with either hand; specifically, carrying a spear in a joust. Also interesting is that in Portugal (in the early XX century and at least until the early 1950's) a child was not allowed to be left-handed! Their teachers forced them, from a very young age, to be right-handed.

As a specific example, my wife currently does most of her chores using preferably her left hand but she was forced to learn how to write using her right hand. Now, from time to time, she enjoys writing also with her left hand. My purely academic question is, was that situation—in Portugal—originated in the Middle Ages?

Chapter III—About some necessary riding skills and how to learn them

In order to be at ease when riding it is necessary to have a good knowledge about all the most important actions you can be required to perform mounted on a beast; otherwise you can neither be at ease nor appear so. I am going to address in the next chapters the actions that are, in my opinion, the most important ones you are required to perform when mounted on a beast and how you should learn them well.

You should train yourself fully armed and wearing your armor (as if you were going to war) and you should participate in jousts and tournaments, having with you good teachers to provide you with all the necessary counseling and warnings, before and after the action.

And it is essential, of course, to believe in and to follow to the letter the instructions and corrective actions you are to receive from them.

Acting similarly you will be able to be at ease when performing several other activities also important when you are mounted on a beast such as galloping up and down hill, hunting, maneuvering and throwing spears[36] and playing with canes and striking with a

---

[36] D. Duarte have used so far only the word *lança*; I have always translated it as **spear** instead of **lance**, for no specific reason (in the Portuguese language we only have the word *lança*); honestly I do not know if there a difference—in English—between the words **spear** and **lance**; I simply prefer *spear*. Starting in the next chapter D. Duarte—namely when in the context of jousts (*justas*) or hunting, sometimes—but not always—uses the word *vara* also as a synonym of *lança* without any apparent reason (at least I could not find any). I have thus translated *vara* also as **spear**.

sword. All these activities should be practiced by all those who want to be at ease when mounted on a beast as it is a known fact that a good and frequent practice is the best of teachers, without which nobody could acquire the necessary skills; and after having achieved that objective it is mandatory to keep practicing, otherwise the skills will be very quickly forgotten.

Keeping up with the objective already announced at the beginning of this chapter I am going to write about other activities that are common when riding to teach those who are not knowledgeable about them (even taking the risk of being contradicted by others). And they are: how to carry the spear (in the hand, at the leg or on the lap); how to maneuver it and use it during a joust; how to throw it correctly and aim well; how to strike with a sword, cut or thrust. The practice of all these activities will make any horseman to feel more at ease on the beast. My writing is the result of the conclusions I took out of my experiences — more than from reason — and I am certain that those who decide to do it in accordance with my advice will see how right I am. And all these activities should not be

Note that *vara* in current Portuguese is not a synonym of *lança* (it is, commonly, just a long — one to two meter or three to six foot — wooden stick), but it looks that it was for D.Duarte — in some occasions — a synonym of *lança*. See the footnote at the end of Chapter XIX (footnote 16) where two different ways of handling and striking with a spear are described; basically keeping the spear horizontal or not (upwards or downwards).

Those two ways are named as follows (in medieval Spanish and Portuguese):

Horizontally – *lança sobre mano* (Spanish) and *lança de sobre-mãao* (Port.)
Non-Horiz.– *lança sobre el braço* (Spanish) and *lança de soo-braço* (Port.)
Starting in the next chapter there are going to occur many references to the handling of the spear (either *sobre-mãao* or *soo-braço*). Whenever that happens I am going to use the original medieval Portuguese terms *sobre-mãao* or *soo-braço*. These two terms (with the respective explanations) are included in the glossary, as are other terms without translation in current Portuguese, which I have also kept in the original.

disdained by the knights and squires who presume that they are not necessary; at the contrary, they all should work hard to learn them well, considering them neither of little importance (and therefore to be disregarded) nor so difficult to master that would not be even worth trying to learn them.

We should all have in mind that to disdain the things that look to be of little importance and to lose all hope of succeeding in the big and difficult ones—finding a justification for that decision—make men simple, with no real incentives and weary of life.

And nobody should feel embarrassed to carry swords at all times, even considering that many, never (or almost never) are going to take any advantage of the decision; even so, they carry them just because they think that sooner or later they might need to use them; their hearts feel light and merry knowing that their owners are skilled in many valuable and good arts, therefore they would have great advantage over others; it is a fact that many have successfully use their various skills in situations of great need and due to that ability are very much respected and highly regarded by all.

Chapter IV—How to carry the spear—de soo-mãao,[37] at the leg and on the lap

In the hand

Following on with the teaching of the various activities necessary to all horsemen, we are now going to address the various ways of carrying the spear when mounted on the beast—de soomãao— at the leg and on the rider's lap.

There are four different ways to carry the spear de soo-mãao:

1. Keeping it horizontal with the arm stretched down

2. Keeping it a bit higher up, resting obliquely over the horse's mane

3. Keeping it resting transversely over the rider's left hand or left arm[38]

4. Keeping it vertical, firmly placed between the rider's belt and his body

In every one of these ways it is absolutely necessary to keep the spear with its center of gravity well placed, ensuring that it stays

---

[37] *Soo-mãao* is the term used by the author and its translation, following its exact words, means only the hand. Actually, the spear is not carried using only the rider's hand but the author wants to emphasize the difference between these ways of carrying a spear and the other two, which involve the legs and the lap of the rider.

[38] Ref. to note Sec. 5, ch. II, footnote 2. D. Duarte assumes the spear is held in the right hand. As noted previously, this happens several times throughout the text.

well balanced in accordance with its weight; it is also mandatory to keep the rider's right arm free to execute, easily and quickly, the movements necessary to throw the spear (which is a light one).

The first way referred above is the most used when the rider is carrying a very lightweight spear. When using the second way, it is necessary to be very careful to avoid the spear to be caught by various obstacles, for example, tree branches. The third way is the best option if the objective is to strike to the left hand side or to the back of the rider. The fourth way is the best and safest way of the four mentioned above to carry a heavier spear.

All this teaching applies when your horse is at a vigorous trot or galloping; otherwise, you can carry your spear the way you like the most because you always have enough time to make any correction eventually required. Nevertheless, if you are travelling over terrain with many trees you should always keep the sharp end of the spear a bit downward; if you are travelling over terrain covered by low brush you should keep the sharp end of your spear a bit upward.

At the leg

The spear is carried vertically; this is the preferred way to carry it around in jousts. The butt of the spear is supported in a small pouch fixed at the rider's leg or at the saddle-bow, depending on the rider's option; and I find it a good and appropriate solution. There are also those who carry the spear tightly squeezed between the leg and the saddle-bow; to be able to take this option they need to be very strong;[39] but if they can do it, they may appear to be at ease

---

[39] This advice is due to the fact that the spears used in jousts (*justas*) and tournaments were very heavy. They were as heavy as possible in accordance with each rider's strength; we will understand that in the next

Whichever solution is used by the rider to carry the spear around during jousts, the spear's shaft should be firmly fixed and in its correct position before the horse starts its final run, charging for the decisive moment of collision and it is an error if you start that final run with the spear's sharp end either vertical or pointing to the left, with your body leaning to the right or to the back. To avoid these errors you should do the contrary of what was just described; you should start that final run with your body firm and your upper body leaning slightly to the left and a little bit forward, holding your spear with its sharp end reasonably low and pointing slightly to the right. I am not giving specific advice about the position of the rider's arms; they are either held tightly to his body or in wider positions as I have already seen every position being successfully and handsomely used. Everyone should use the solution he likes the most, considering the results he already achieved with it and which he also knows to be praised by many. Nevertheless, they should not forget all the errors I have already identified in the carrying of the spear, because I did it based on my experience; in my opinion they are neither beneficial nor look good to the ones who are unable to avoid them.

On the lap

The following errors might occur when you carry the spear on your lap:

• The middle point of the spear on your lap

• The spear's sharp end pointing upwards

• The rider's hand near his shoulder

---

chapter when the author describes the teaching methodology for the choice of a spear for a *justa* or tournament

• The rider's hand in front of his face

• The rider's elbow kept low

The riders who want to act correctly should just do the contrary:

• Place the point of the spear's shaft by which you want to handle it (or slightly near to the spear's sharp end, in accordance with the spear's weight) on the center of your lap

• The spear's sharp end should be kept reasonably low

• The rider's hand should be far from his shoulder

• The rider's hand should be kept on the side of his body

• The rider's elbow should be kept high

A rider who does as I say will feel at ease and will be more efficient — or handsome — whether wearing his body armor or not.

Chapter V—Teaching how to maneuver the spear[40]

Training should be done at first with the student standing on his feet (not mounted) and quiet and all the instructions should be exemplified using a light weight spear or a wooden stick, as it is easier to ensure that the correct actions are performed if we are maneuvering a light weight spear. The main instructions to achieve a correct maneuvering of a spear are the following:

At first, how to hold the spear in its most frequent initial position, vertical, near to our leg; we should have it firmly held in our hand with our arm stretched down.

---

[40] Due to its eventual length and lack of revision, this chapter—in the original work—was not organized at it should be. For example, D. Duarte switches sometimes from one subject to the other without any specific reference and also
comes back to subjects already addressed to add further points. It is sometimes
not immediately clear if D. Duarte is speaking about maneuvering light-weight spears or heavy-weight ones. Readers should be able to understand—without great difficulty—by the description of the movements, if it is light or heavy.
To ensure an easier understanding of D. Duarte's ideas and advices, I feel compelled to change the sequence of some descriptions; I tried, as much as possible, to collect within the whole chapter all the bits and pieces belonging to the same subject, and I put them all together and in what I hope is a reasonable sequence. This being said, let's go back to the main text having in mind that D. Duarte is going to concentrate himself (in this chapter) in the maneuvering of the heavy spears, those used in jousts. The descriptions that follow assume that the student is already mounted. And we should not forget that the title of this chapter is *Teaching How to Maneuver the Spear* and that D. Duarte, as he usually does, addresses the reader directly.

As I just said the student should start learning to maneuver a light weight spear and its size and weight should be progressively increased until the maximum weight the student can correctly maneuver is defined.[41]

Nobody should attempt to use spears weighting more than what he is physically capable of handling as it can produce such consequences as hernias, pain in the back, head, legs and hands without any benefit.

And as soon you have learned to maneuver a spear while not mounted on the beast, you should start trying it mounted, going around slowly to prove to yourself you can do it and also to enable your teacher to correct you whenever necessary and appropriate. And this is of the utmost importance because nobody is able to achieve the right attitude and act correctly in the art of riding if he is not taught and corrected from the beginning. And the rider should progressively increase the beast's pace until he feels at ease in a strong gallop; then he will understand the great advantage he holds over others who are unable to match his skills.

Due to the great weight of the spear, the first step is to take it out of its vertical position and this should be done with a violent thrust of your arm and hand, raising the spear onto your breast; this being done, your hand should immediately glide along the spear's shaft, stretching your arm and enabling you to sustain the spear's weight for a while; then, you move your hand in the direction of your arm (though, to the back) and encase the spear's butt in the *restre*;[42] be

---

[41] This teaching methodology shows how important was to be able to use very heavy spears in jousts; the heavier, the better.

[42] *Restre* — piece of iron on the breastplate of the rider's armour to support the spear's butt when couched for charging (spear rest). For the maneuvering of light weight spears there is no need of a restre (actually, we could say that the rider's hand *is* the restre). For the maneuvering of

also aware that you should hold the spear in the palm of your hand with your fingers firmly around it and not just with your fingers because, if you do that, the spear will probably slip out of them due to its great weight.

If you do not use a real restre you can use your armpit as an alternative when the spear is kept well balanced due to three support points, namely your armpit (with your arm tightly connected to your upper body), the lateral part of your breast (against which the spear's shaft is positioned) and your hand. And this way you have the spear under your control (and in a horizontal position, if that is your objective), firmly squeezed between your chest and your arm; and you should keep your body erect and act as elegantly as possible. And if you want to move the spear from its initial vertical position onto your lap you should also do it with a violent thrust of your arm and pull of your hand; but you should not forget immediately after that to put your arm in the correct position it should be whenever you are carrying the spear on your lap (as I said before). If you have an *arondella*[43] fixed in your spear's shaft, be aware of its relative position; if it is near your lap, it is not only ugly but you can also hurt yourself if are not wearing your body armor.

More Advice:

It is always advantageous to ride against the wind, leaving the control of the beast to your left hand; you should not allow the

---

heavy weight spears there is a need of a restre on the rider's breastplate with the rider's hand acting as a second restre, such is the spear's weight

[43] *Arondella*—guard firmly fixed to the spear's shaft to protect the rider's hand (with the same objective as the guards of modern swords).

sharp end of your spear to fall down under the level of your head;[44] in case this starts to happen, do not allow it to happen suddenly: hold the spear's weight with your arm and hand and use your strength to replace the spearback to its correct position.

If your spear has a *gozete*[45] put your hand or at least one of your fingers over it, either if you are riding with or without a restre (it is easier to maneuver the spear if you have both—the restre and the gozete).

Do not forget to start maneuvering the spear from its initial vertical position using a violent thrust of your arm and pulling with your hand to raise the spear on to your breast; one additional warning on this subject: use your elbow to help support the spear until you are able to encase it in the restre and use the strength of your hand to keep the spear from falling down suddenly rather, raise the sharp end of the spear more than the required height and then allow it to

---

[44] I should elaborate a bit to avoid what might look, at first glance, like some contradictory advice from D. Duarte (because in other part of his book, D. Duarte writes that you should keep your spear point low). The advisable position of the sharp end of your spear depends on several things: how you are carrying the spear (in the hand, at the leg or on the lap), if you are traveling against the wind, if you are crossing land covered by many trees or by low brush wood. An example of one apparent contradiction: If you are against (or with) the wind through a land with many trees, you should carry your spear with its sharp end a bit downward (to avoid the tree branches); if you are against the wind through a low brush wood land, you should carry the sharp end of your spear a bit upward. Basically, there are many specific situations you can face and so, the most advisable carrying position for your spear varies accordingly

[45] *Gozete*—specific piece fixed to the spear's shaft (made of iron or leather) to ensure a better grip, keeping the rider's hand from slipping and consequently losing its grip on the correct point of the shaft.

go slowly down to the correct position. Whenever you are galloping at strong pace, with or without restre, you should make sure — in case you carry the spear at the leg — that you keep the spear firm against the saddle and keep your body quiet.

If you carry the spear de soo-braço, you should have it strongly grasped in your hand and do not allow its sharp end to fall down.

If you are galloping against the wind, you should not carry the spear with its sharp end too high; you should also keep the spear tightly squeezed against your own body, holding it still and you should put — as soon as possible — the spear in the right position and direction for the collision.

In accordance with our custom — if you are galloping carrying the spear at the leg — you should keep your feet firm in the stirrups, squeeze your legs against the horse's body, move your body along with the cadence of the horse's movements and bumps; only then should you lift the spear, encase it in the restre and acquire the correct position of carrying the spear de soo-braço, as already described. And those who decide to follow all these instructions will find themselves riding more handsomely and at ease.

And I am going to repeat some of my reasons — and to mention some more — to ensure that they are better understood; this is because I consider that it is more important to be sure that everything is well understood than to produce a very elegant text.

If you are maneuvering the spear with your hand close to its sharp end and are not using a restre, and want to move your spear to its position at the leg, you should squeeze the spear's shaft between the lateral part of your breast and your arm.

If you are using a restre, press the spear's shaft with your arm and elbow, encase it in the restre and do not forget to use your hand to keep the spear's sharp end from falling down under a certain height.

There are some who say that it is better to carry the spear resting on the left arm; they say that they put it in striking position quicker and also that they strike better to their left and to their back.

When the spear is carried on the right shoulder, some allow it to fall down over the right arm as a way of being able to protect their back quicker; others allow the spear's sharp end to fall down to the ground and recover it back to their shoulder for further maneuvers.

All these ways of maneuvering a spear are very useful to know as they could be used in times of need; those who know them all are riding more at ease than the others.

But I am not going to write about things I consider with no interest— such as maneuvering two or three spears simultaneously or handling them above the head; even so, I consider that those who do such things, feel and are at ease.

In summary (and in which concerns the carrying of the spear de soobraço) the following errors can be made, namely:

• Carrying a spear that is too heavy, though you are unable to maneuver it correctly and may even fall down with it

• Leaning the body too much to the right[46]

• Not being quiet on the saddle (feet, legs, head, body, spear)

• Carrying the spear at too much of an angle, or pointing too much to the outside or too high or too low

---

[46] D. Duarte assumes a right handed rider. Reading carefully through the whole book there are many more situations where this assumption is evident.

• Positioning the head and the rider's face too close to the spear

• Positioning the rider's head too high and leaning to the back

And to do everything right, the rider just needs to avoid all these errors.

As far as jousts are concerned it is most important to use the spurs correctly, which is not as easy as it looks. Some riders are using the spurs continuously—from the starting of the final run until the moment of collision. This is not only ugly but it also makes the rider weaker; actually, in these situations we should use the spurs as few times as possible, strongly or lightly in accordance with the beast's temper. And the appropriate moments to use the spurs are only two: to start the final run (to get from the beast the proper galloping pace) and just a moment before the collision (when we have the spear already aiming at the other jouster). From that moment onwards we should keep our feet and legs very quiet and firm until the collision happens; this assumes the beast behaves as it should; if it gets wild and changes direction, the rider must use all the appropriate means to correct the situation, including the use of the spurs.

In our jousts there are riders who prefer to maneuver the spear using the left hand. About this I say that everyone should have his own specific techniques; if a technique is well practiced, the hand, the arm and the body get used to it and eventually master it with the necessary good results. Let us consider as examples a string instrument player who is used to play using the fingers of one of his hands and a bird-hunter who favors one hand; they are both unable to do it correctly with the other hand (even knowing how it should be done).

Therefore we can see the importance for everyone of us to know how to use our own body to master any specific art or technique; we need not only to get the necessary knowledge how one thing should be done but we have to practice it at length (which is the only way to master it). Final Advice and Considerations

There is one important piece of advice to be considered whenever we are maneuvering a big and heavy spear and we are not wearing our body armor; and I give this advice because that's what I always do in those circumstances:

• When I raise the spear from its initial vertical position, I allow my hand to glide for a while along the spear's shaft and with this technique the impact of the spear's weight when it falls down on my shoulder is reduced. Acting this way, I am able to stay quieter and at ease on the saddle and I think that this technique might be a big advantage for those who learn well how to use it.

• There are those who — even knowing how to maneuver a spear — feel embarrassed when doing it, either because their armor is not of good quality and does not fit them as it should, or the restre or the braçal [47]disturbs them, or they did not ensure that all the horse's harness — namely the interlaced ropes tying the stirrups underneath the horses belly — were properly prepared and fixed. Though, it is absolutely necessary that, before they start to participate in jousts, they train as many times as they need, until they feel at ease. For example, they should train several times to encase the spear's butt in the restre until they are sure they can do it correctly without feeling disturbed or embarrassed. And Dom Duarte's *Livro da Ensinança de Bem Cavalgar Toda Sela* after several days of training they should also do it wearing their full body armor under conditions similar to the ones they are going to face in the future; and every single detail should be taken care of, including training to

---

[47] *Braçal* — protective armor for the rider's arms.

maneuver the spear to its final position, charging to the collision. (Details about the moment of collision are the objective of the next chapter.)

And those who decide to train not wearing their full body armor, should pay attention to every detail that might embarrass or disturb them in action, such as the clothes they wear—namely the doublet's sleeves (too tight or too loose)—which might cause them difficulties to correctly position their spear de soo-braço.

Finally, after feeling that all the details were duly checked and trained and that you are prepared for action, do not forget that, above everything, you must have a good horse; without it, all the knowledge you have and the preparations you have done are of very small value.

Chapter VI—Teaching how to act at the moment of collision

I am going to write down instructions I consider good and reasonable to enable all riders to act as they should at the moment of collision (in jousts and when hunting) and I hope that they would be taken into consideration by all those who want to avoid making the most common errors. In this chapter I am going to address the jousts—because they are the more important of the two situations.

Men are not acting as they should at the moment of collision, due to four main reasons:

Poor sighting, incorrect maneuvering of the spear, problems related to their horses and lack of a safe and strong will.[48],[49]

---

[48] The first two reasons are to be discussed during this chapter; the third, in the next chapter (chapter VII); the fourth, is the objective of chapters VIII to

Poor sighting

Some make mistakes because they close their eyes at the moment of collision, without even realizing it! Others are aware of it but they are unable to avoid it. Others, because they have the helmet or the shield wrongly placed, are unable to see the other jouster at the moment of collision due to the horse's jolting movements even at a steady gallop.

There are those who — in the attempt to see the other jouster — move their eyes inside their heads and their heads inside their helmets, but in most cases that is not enough; in order to see — again — the other jouster, they also need to rotate their upper body by the waist, before the collision happens. The best way for a jouster to fix all these possible errors is to have with him a spotter [50] knowledgeable in this art who, after each collision happens, starts asking the jouster why he thinks he succeeded or failed. Actually, it frequently happens that — especially if there was a violent collision — the jouster doesn't know what really happened and the spotter must be able to tell the jouster that he was not looking at his opponent at the

---

X. As to hunting using a spear (referred by D. Duarte at the beginning of this chapter), it will be the focus of chapters XI to XIII.

[49] I feel that D. Duarte really should have been concerned with giving the readers a real sequence of the various subjects he was going to address and their distribution throughout the various chapters. I felt forced to read the 2nd half of the book before restart translating it, to understand what was he really going to cover, how and when.

[50] A solution used today in several sports such as weightlifting or gymnastics.

moment of collision and should force him to correct this major error.

Nevertheless, when the jouster really has closed his eyes without realizing it, it is more difficult to correct and the spotter should be allowed (and entitled) to tell the jouster in a very plain-spoken way not only that error but also all the other errors he identified; the jouster, feeling angry and annoyed with himself would then have the proper incentive he needs to correct himself.

As an example, if he has failed two or three times because he aimed the spear in the other jouster's direction too late, he should be told to do it earlier during the final run; actually, it might happen that, even not seeing the other jouster as he should, he might be lucky and his spear might find the adversary just because he had enough time to change the spear's direction; the pleasure of having making contact with the adversary once, might be enough to give the jouster the necessary strong will to keep his eyes well open!

A jouster might also lose sight of his adversary due to a wrong preparation of his body armor; one possible way of correcting this error is the following:

Being already mounted wearing your full body armor, put the spear de soo-braço and ensure the proper fitting of the helmet and the shield doing the following: keep the spear correctly positioned for the collision and even considering the eventual movements of the helmet and the shield due to the normal jolting at the gallop ensure that—up to the moment of collision—you always see half (or at least the last third) of your spear. If you cannot achieve that objective immediately, you should train it as many times as needed because you have to be able to do it; it is a fact that, one who cannot see properly, cannot be in the best possible condition at the moment of collision!

To ensure the correct position of the helmet and the best possible eyesight through it, it is in my opinion better to fix it first in the back and only then in the front; acting this way, the helmet stays better fixed and it is better for your eyesight than to do the contrary.

To ensure the best possible view of your adversary at the moment of collision, you should have your body positioned directly facing him throughout all your run along the *tea*[51] and right before the collision you should turn your head also directly to him, to see him face-to-face through the helmet, and not obliquely. This is the way to have the best possible sight of your adversary at the moment of collision.

---

[51] *Tea* (*teia* in modern Portuguese) — the barrier that separates either the joust field from the spectators and/or the jousters between themselves. In English, sometimes called a "tilt barrier." *Taille* in the French; there are records indicating that it was a Portuguese introduction into Burgundy during the 15th century; previously there was no barrier.

Comments about the *tea* – In a Portuguese Encyclopaedia we have, there is a reproduction of an illumination of a joust between Nicolau Clifford (an English rider) and a French rider. Its author is Jean Wavrin, XV century, and the original is part of the British Museum collection, in London. The riders are shown at the moment of collision and there is no *tea* (barrier) between them; there are two parallel gratings at both sides of the joust field, separating it from the spectators.

It is clear in D. Duarte's descriptions of jousts — the Portuguese way — that there was always a long *tea* separating the riders during the final run against each other. They started their final run to the moment of collision from opposite ends of the joust field and from opposite sides of the *tea*; so, they were always separated from each other by the *tea* during their final run to the moment of collision.

Wrong maneuver of the spear

There are also four main reasons why you make errors in the maneuvering of the spear during a joust:

o **First** — Bad quality of the body armor — namely of the braçal — or bad preparation and placement of the restre, the shield, the arondella or the gozete.

o **Second** — The spear is too heavy.

o **Third** — The jouster is not quiet and at ease on the saddle.

o **Fourth** — The horse becomes so wild that it is impossible to control it using the bridle.

Let's address each one of them (looking for the solution):

First — The solution is obtained through training and rehearsals — as many times as needed — until the jouster can ensure that he is not going to be embarrassed by any piece of his armor during the joust. And before going to the tea to start the final run, put your spear two or three times de soo-braço to ensure that everything is at it should and that you feel yourself at ease.

Second — The jouster should ensure that he is not using a spear too heavy (in accordance with his own strength).

Third — Quietness and easiness are obtained through practice and knowledge of the art of riding, as I said before. I am adding a few additional instructions: ensure that the interlaced ropes tying the stirrups underneath the horse's belly are not too tight; ensure that the saddle is neither too loose not too tight; ensure that the shape of the saddle's flap has an adequate hollow for the jouster's legs; ensure that the saddle's seat is neither too long nor too short and is well padded. After all these things are ensured, the jousters should feel themselves at ease, calm and in control of their horses and their spears.

Fourth — The horse is to be controlled by the jouster using the bridle, the reins and the spurs; it should not be disobedient, unquiet or acting with malice, embarrassing the jouster. There are partial solutions for some of the problems just referred, like the use of a stronger bridle (but not too strong, as the horse might raise his head too much or put it in between its hands) and wearing spurs with less, shorter and not too sharp spikes.

In my opinion, it is not the task of the jouster's servants to bring him the horse by the reins, using wooden sticks to control it or even wounding it if they feel the need for it; at the contrary, it is the task of the jousters to pick up their horses, to control them using the reins and the spurs, and to train them galloping along the tea, closer or more distant, in accordance with the horse's temper.

If the riders do not do all these things themselves, very few would be able to correctly maneuver the spears and become good jousters, even if their horses have a strong and even paced gallop and have a *cabeçada*[52] on their heads, enabling the jouster to carry his spear very quietly (after it is duly placed in the restre).

---

[52] *Cabeçada* — specific headgear of a horse's harness made of the same fabric as the girths; it might include *antolhos* (small squares of leather or thick cloth fixed around the horse's eyes making impossible for the horse to see sideways, so reducing the horse's level of anxiety and fear); in the original text, D. Duarte mentions that horses wearing *enxácomas* have a better behavior; having in consideration the sentence and the context in which the word *enxácomas* is included in the original text, it is my understanding that *enxácomas* might be the above referred *antolhos* (this means that I consider the XV century word *enxácomas*, which I could not find anywhere, to have the same objective as the current *antolhos*).

Chapter VII—Teaching how to control, guide and direct the horse during a joust

The objective of this chapter is to identify in detail and to correct the errors in managing the horses during a joust (which was the third main reason for making errors at the moment of collisions referred in the last chapter).

The main reasons why men might not handle correctly their horses during jousts are four:

First—The jousters do not use the reins properly, therefore do not control the bridle as they should; as a direct consequence of this error the horses are left on their own, uncontrolled, and it is impossible for them to be correctly managed as they need to be at the always difficult moment of collision. Even if the horse's harness includes *taris*[53] bridles and very good reins, the fact is of no importance, if the jouster doesn't use the reins properly.

Second—The reins are cut or broken or have no *barbella*;[54] as a consequence, the jousters are unable to properly control their horses as the reins have no action over the bridle.

Third—The jousters, to feel themselves very firm on the horses at the moment of collision, fit additional ropes on the horse. (Those ropes come either from the horse's face or from its girth and go through between the horse's hands to the jouster's hands.) The

---

[53] *Taris*—type of bridle that is part of the harness commonly used with de Gineta saddles.

[54] *Barbella*—curb chain underneath the horse's inferior lip, linked to the bridle (and consequently to the reins).

jousters are so determined to use that additional advantage that they forget to use the reins to control the horse.

Fourth — The jousters handle and control the horses as they should, using the reins and the bridle but when the horses are at gallop in their final run towards the collision, are not close enough to the *tea* and the jouster, due to lack of knowledge and/or correct counselling, is unable to force the horse to gallop close to the *tea* in time for the collision; so, the collision might not happen at all.

We are now going to describe how the jouster should act to avoid all the errors just referred:

First — When you are training, hold the reins before putting on your body armour and chose their correct length to enable you to force your horse to the appropriate gallop's pace for the joust. Then, make a knot on the reins to mark their correct length and go on training to ensure you did it correctly. Do it all over again with your body armour on.   a bit biomechanical ?

Whenever you find a difference (reins too short, too long or of different lengths) make the necessary correction. You can achieve this (ensure the reins are with the appropriate length) in three ways:

1. Making a knot on them, as it was already described

2. Using a *travinca* and making the knot with the reins around it

3. Additionally to 2. (and with the travinca still in your hand) wind the reins around your hand (one turn only). Doing it this way you can — if you feel the need for it — rapidly unwind the reins from your hand and keep only the travinca in your hand.

If a jouster did not prepare the reins before he can still do it when riding to the joust field. This is the way it should be done:

The jouster holds the reins as he thinks he should, uses the spurs to force the horse to gallop and then stops it using the reins, moving one hand at a time; if he is a good horseman he knows if the reins were too short, too long or of different lengths and so, he can make the appropriate correction.

To make the correction—even if he is already wearing his helmet, the jouster takes out his *gante*[55] (or his right hand glove) puts his hand in the correct point of the reins and asks one of his helpers to just make the knot on them or around the travinca (if that was the jouster's option).

And acting as I have just described the jouster will avoid the first reason for the errors that might happen when managing a horse during a joust —not using the reins properly—for which it is necessary that both have the appropriate length).

Second—To joust the Portuguese way, the rider should ensure that the bridle is fitted on the horse in a way that it is easy to control it, using the reins the rider holds in his hand. The bridle should not be too tight or too loose but in a position that it becomes easy for the jouster to force the horse to be closer or more distant to the *tea* in accordance with the required by each situation. And those who do it right, will be able to see the great advantage they hold over others whose horses have no barbellas or have the bridles fitted in a way that doesn't enable the riders to control them properly with the reins.

Third—Having in mind those who do not pay the necessary attention to the reins (and to their action over the bridle) due to the importance they give to the additional reins they fitted on the

---

[55] *Gante*—iron glove (gauntlet)

horse's faces or to the girths, this is the way to avoid those errors and to handle the reins during the joust as it should be:

After having done the corrective action described earlier — marking the correct points in the reins with the knot and the travinca, if you have decided to use it — you then put on your body armor, take the additional ropes and tied them up in some specific point of your body, keeping the reins in your hand; it is of the utmost importance that the length of the ropes is greater than the length of the reins, so as not to embarrass the horse's movements.

This way you can gain advantage not only from the reins you hold in your hand but also from the additional ropes[56] that can help you to stay mounted on the horse whenever there are violent collisions (this assumes that the additional ropes are allowed by those specific joust's rules).

Fourth — I have seen jousters fail the collision, because the horses were not close enough to the *tea*, mainly for two reasons:

• Some riders do not pay enough attention and their horses are always too far from the *tea*.

• Some riders, with the objective of acquiring advantage over the other jouster, have their horses galloping too distant from the *tea* and when they force them to change direction towards the *tea* and

angle of incident

---

[56] It is interesting to note that these additional ropes are still used in the Portuguese bullfights whenever the rider tries to perform a difficult (but not very common) trick that consists in trying to put a pair of *bandarilhas* on the bull; because the rider needs both hands to perform the trick, he uses, just for that trick, those additional ropes tied to a specific point on his body to have additional firmness on the saddle. Note that he is only allowed to use them for that trick (which in fact always generates strong reactions, positive and negative, from the spectators).

[143]

their adversary, they are late; so, when they get there, their adversary has already passed through (and no collision happens!).

There are two ways of avoiding these errors:

1. Even if it looks to you that your horse is galloping too close to the *tea*, keep it in that direction and keep its head directly facing the adversary; acting in this way you are sure to have some advantage at the moment of collision (if your adversary does not do the same).

2. Understanding your error of having your horse galloping too far from the *tea*, you have to correct its direction sooner, enabling you to get closer to the *tea* at the moment of collision or preferably, before it.

Due to the fact that only few jousters are really aware of their own limitations and errors, it is most advantageous always to have a friendly spotter during the jousts to discuss with you—after the event—what did really happen.

Acting in these ways, the jouster will be able correctly to manage his horse during a joust, which is one of the main things every jouster needs to know.

Chapter VIII — The four driving wills in human beings and the consequences for their behavior[57]

Speaking about the safety represented by the strong will that is necessary to be successful in a joust (the last of the four reasons mentioned at the beginning of chapter VI) I confess I feel pleasure in allowing my mind to wander and daydream around areas involving the will and also to give some teaching to those who do not have great knowledge about these things.

First of all, be aware that there are four driving wills in the Human Beings; they are more or less in permanent conflict with each other and the outcome of it influences decisively the human beings' behavior in every situation (this is clearly described in a book I consider a great authority on this subject).[58]

First — Carnal

Second — Spiritual

Third — Pleasant and Half-hearted

Fourth — Perfect and Virtuous (Obedient to good reason and

understanding)

---

[57] This chapter, with slight changes and variations, is the chapter 3 in one of Duarte's other works, *Leal Conselheiro* (Loyal Advisor).

[58] This is derived in part from the *Conferences* of John Cassian, a fifth century monastic work concerned with sin and the human will. See esp. Conferences 4, 9 and 12.

The *First* will wants to satiate lewdness, pursue the recreation of the body, and be wary and run away from anything that might represent danger, expense and work.

The *Second* will wants to practice all the virtues that are part of a religious person namely to fast, to wake, to read and to pray as much as possible and without any limitation. And those who abide by the ideals of chivalry and behave in accordance with this will expose themselves to all dangers and tasks, forgetting to take any protective measures.

As an example, that happens when performing certain deeds they consider to be good and virtuous; they dedicate themselves to them so intensely that they forget to eat, sleep and rest their bodies as much as nature requires. And if there are expenses to be incurred, they pay them without any care for the consequences to their assets.

These two wills already described are — inside us — in permanent conflict against each other; for sure, we all already have had the experience of situations where one of these wills was counseling us to do a certain thing and the other was advising us to do the contrary.

Between these two wills — says the book I have mentioned — there is a *Third* one, pleasant and half-hearted which, due to the fact that it wants to please the other two without offending either of them, puts those persons who follow this third will in such a situation that they neither live well (in accordance with the first will) nor virtuously (in accordance with the second will); as an example, the third will would advise a person to do such things as to fast when he is neither thirsty nor hungry or to wake when there is no danger in sleep; this third will also aims at such things as enabling a person to be honored by his chivalric deeds without having to run through any risks or overcome hard and difficult obstacles or to get the reputation of being generous without having made any expenditures that could represent any difficulty to him.

These examples really show that the objective of this third will is to fulfill the needs of one of the two first wills without antagonizing the other.

The *Fourth* will — perfect and virtuous — doesn't always follow what any of the other three want and a person who acts in accordance with this fourth will, does — many times — what the other three dislike; this is achieved based on a strong determination and the overruling of one's good reason and understanding. That's why there is a saying: To follow a will[59] is to fulfill its wickedness; to defeat it is a great virtue.

And all this happens in the following way:

If a man lives in accordance with any of the first three wills being unable to act through the imposition of the fourth will — the good reason and understanding — over the other three, for sure he will lose his soul and body; this is so because the first will asks for things so vile and worthless which manifestly expose the man to all vices; the second will wants to pursue objectives so ambitious and beyond any reasonable limits that they might result in death, sickness or loss of all his assets; the third will, because it wants to agree and please the other two, would never be able to persuade us to do anything of value and beneficial. In conclusion, the fulfillment of any of these first three wills represent to us nothing but big mistakes and misdeeds.

The fourth will is the opposite of the first three; because everything the first three wills put to the consideration of our heart, is to be

---

[59] Evidently the author is considering any of the first three wills already described.

proposed to our good reason and understanding, for decision. And that is why many times we do not do any of the things required by the first three wills, or we do things that are contrary to their interests or neither. As a comparison, the fourth will acts like a goldsmith when anyone wants to sell him gold or silver; he tests the gold's quality with cement and the silver's quality with lye[60] and only then he decides whether to buy; the fourth will also decides to approve or not the doing of a specific thing in accordance with the result of scrutiny by our understanding and good reason.

When the carnal will wants to satisfy its objectives, the fourth will might be strong enough not to accept it and instead might order a person to suffer from hunger, thirst, sleep or to go through great dangers, expenses and troubles, if that is what it should be done in accordance with reason.

A similar thing happens to the second will, which might see its objectives denied by the fourth will, if they are too ambitious and dangerous in accordance with the person's specific situation and wealth.

---

[60] This is nice basic applied chemistry in the Middle Ages! *Lye* is a strong alkaline solution (produced in the Middle Ages by boiling water with vegetable ashes) and it was mainly used to wash clothes; it dissolves all the salts and oxides that are on the silver's surface giving back to it the known silver's shininess. Cement is, by definition, a mixture of substances that become very hard after drying; for sure the composition of the cement of the XV century had nothing to see (in common) with the current industrial cement; so, I have no way to understand how a XV century goldsmith could identify the quality of the gold using cement (and gold is an element very difficult to react to any other substance), but it should have been something that produced a very straightforward identification of the gold element; perhaps based on physics and not chemistry (like the gold's high density of 19).

This is a basic difference between the fourth and the third wills: the third will would never opposes any of the first two; the fourth will would take that decision if it considers it as the correct thing to do.

And contrary to the first two wills, it is most important for the reason (the fourth will) to know what should be done in every case and situation whenever the first two wills are fighting between them; this happens in the following way (as an example):

If the second will requires excessive fasting and the first will is for the immediate satisfaction of the pleasures of the body — presenting as argumentation, the dangers that might be consequences of the fast — there is a fight between these two wills. This gives the fourth will (the reason) the time to analyze the situation and to define the correct action to be taken, what would have been impossible without the fight between the first two wills.[61]

This situation happens neither to those who live without any restraint according to the requests coming from the first will, nor to the ones who have the presumption and pride themselves upon their ability to oppose the carnal desires without difficulty; actually, total submission to the demands coming from the second will could also cause great falls and damage, as it is shown by many examples.

Having written all this, some who did not have enough knowledge about these subjects do understand now the various wills that are permanently influencing our behavior and why we should not follow the requests from the first three wills but instead, accept the fourth will — our mind's good reasoning power and understanding — as the ultimate factor in the decision about what we should do.

---

[61] Very interesting, and naïve, by the author, to give a time dimension to the fight among wills; certainly, to make the explanation easier to describe and to be understood.

And when I mention the reason and the understanding, I might not be referring to ours; they might come from those who, having more knowledge, practice and experience than us about the situations we are facing, give us advice we should follow.

This is the way to go; in our language we call it the way of true wisdom, which is highly praised by the knowledgeable ones and who brings to all those who follow it—under God—all good, repelling all evil.

This fourth will –good reason and understanding—is the real cause for our choices of the good instead of evil, of the greatest of the good things and of the smallest of the evil things.

Chapter IX—*The virtues we need to practice to be able to refuse the first three wills, accepting the fourth*[62]

To write in accordance with what it is expected in a treatise about the art of riding on horseback I can say that we need three bridles to avoid following the interests of the first three wills, being therefore able to act in accordance with the fourth.

The **first** bridle—is the fear of the pains of hell and of the existing laws passed by those who have that power over us The **second** bridle—is the wish for rewards/recompenses to be received during this life on earth and in the other, for having always done good deeds, and run away from evil

---

[62] This chapter, with slight changes and variations, is Chapter 5 of *Leal Conselheiro* (Loyal Advisor).

The **third** bridle – is our love of God[63] and of the virtues

The *first* bridle is the fear represented by FAITH itself (referred in the book I have already mentioned in the last chapter); we believe that if we do evil things, we will suffer the appropriate punishment.

The *second* bridle is HOPE, which makes us to believe that, if we live virtuously, we will receive, under God, great rewards.

The *third* bridle is CHARITY, by which we love God above everything; so, we practice all virtues to please Him, refusing all which is contrary to them, as we do not want to displease He Whom we love above everything.

And not forgetting that, each one of these virtues (FAITH, HOPE and CHARITY) is by itself enough to guide us through a clear and straight life (which is only followed by few), there is a big difference among them; the first two belong to those who start and carry on with a way of life whose objectives are to achieve more perfection; the third one belongs to those who, not acting anymore as slaves who serve and obey because they fear the punishment, raise themselves to the condition of servants who expect to be rewarded by their good work and from there to the status of good and loyal sons that consider all his FATHER'S wishes as their own. And they do not serve, honor and fear the FATHER because they are afraid of being punished or hope to receive rewards but because they feel a true love; so, they are afraid of hurting him Whom they love very much and as a consequence, to lose the FATHER'S love. And this love stays forever, because those who feel that love inside them, are not concerned with being far away, because if you love Him totally, you feel His presence everywhere; and for this reason, they are able to avoid doing things that are contrary to His pleasure.

---

[63] I took the decision to write some words in capital letters; they are not written that way in the original text.

And hope should exist abundantly because those who feel a greater love also feel a stronger desire and so they expect to receive more; this is the reason why hope should be a cultivated virtue.

And to those who start serving only due to the fear of being punished, it could happen that their desire and love, joining other good things, become stronger; that will reduce or even will make the strength of the fear disappear.

And to those who expect to receive a reward, the love of another good thing could grow stronger, becoming more important than the reward they were waiting for.

And those who love with their hearts, with all their will and strength will have everything inside them. Nevertheless they cannot do things contrary to the object of their love; that love would eventually die if they acted against the reasons why that love exists.

Besides all this, the love of the three virtues and the habit of their practice restrains the practice of evil and sins which are many times linked to the first three aforementioned wills possessed by human beings and consequently helps human beings to act in accordance with the fourth will—good reason and understanding.

And I wrote all this—even recognizing that there is much more to write about this subject—to help those who do not have great knowledge of it. That was the reason why I have used the concept of the three bridles that every one of us should carry inside his heart to feel and to know his virtues in a much better way than the way I have used to describe them.

Chapter X—How errors are made by those who are involved in jousts due to a confusion of the wills

On the subject of safety of the jousters, and the lack of it, they might make mistakes for four main reasons:

First—Because they do not really want to joust with the other rider.

Second—Because they are stiff with fear and so, they are very uncomfortable at the moment of collision.

Third—Because they move their bodies and spears too much, being too anxious for the moment of collision.

Fourth—Because they want always to have advantages over the other jouster and as a consequence of it, they are likely to make mistakes.

Let's discuss each one of these reasons (and situations) in more detail:

First—Some fail the collision deliberately. There are various possible reasons for that decision: they consider the other jouster too strong; they have a horse too weak or they are handling a spear too thick.

So, recognizing the advantage of the opponent, they want to avoid defeat. This situation falls under the scope of the fourth will referred in the chapter VIII (perfect and virtuous, obeying to the reason and understanding), as the jouster is just obeying to his reason ; he doesn't want to lose and will avoid the opponent unless his understanding gives him another opinion, convincing him to joust.

Others fail the collision falling under the scope of the carnal will which wants total safety and to be far away from any danger and work. And this happens as follows:

The rider initially has the intention to joust; he gets the spear and starts galloping for the collision but when he is closing in there is a wicked will which starts counseling him—against his initial decision—to run away from the collision; this fight between wills goes on up to the moment of collision and it is many times won by the wicked will; whenever that happens, the rider aborts the collision, abruptly changing the positions of his body and spear. It might happen that the rider gets angry with himself for having failed the collision and comes back to correct his behavior, restarting his final run to the collision, again with the intention of succeeding. Many times the situation occurs all over again, because the rider's free will chooses again the counseling of the weak and ill natured will and not the strong and virtuous.

And this is the main reason why we sin; whenever that happens, it is either for this reason or due to our own negligence. Before a decisive moment, our good will is strong and full of determination to do what we should but when the moment comes, our free will — which was before in agreement with our good will—changes its position and convinces us to run away from any danger or eventually accepts as good any other justification given by our ill-natured will; so, it is said that whenever we sin, it is either due to the ignorance of our understanding, which is unable to give us right counseling before the moment of decision or because our free will takes the worse decision, believing that it is the better and the safer one.

Second—Being stiff with fear and uncomfortable at the moment of collision falls under the scope of the carnal will. But there is a difference between this situation and the one just discussed:

In the first situation, the riders decide at the moment of collision to abort it and deliberately change the direction of the spear to avoid the collision. In this second situation, the riders are so afraid that they tighten their bodies to feel themselves more firm, close their eyes and miss the collision; or, the tightening of their arms against their bodies' changes the direction of the spear, with the same end result.

And all this is clearly due to the first will, which wants total safety.

Third — those who make mistakes due to too much haste and do not spend enough time in the proper preparation of their bodies and spears, fall under the scope of the second will which I named spiritual. As an example, that situation might happen with the crossbowmen who do not spend enough time preparing their crossbows and do not make the correct shots; as a result, the arrows go off in every possible direction. And some of them, even having the understanding of their mistakes, are unable to correct them.

Fourth — There are those who are good jousters but try to look not so good to have the opportunity to joust against weaker jousters; they are the ones that might make mistakes just because, being aware of their advantage, they might disregard some important aspects such as: not properly evaluating his opponent or not preparing the horses or the weapons as they should.

We know that the first will wants to avoid all dangers and work but would not find any pleasure (one of its important objectives) in the situation aforementioned, due to the existing advantage over the opponent.

We know that the second will, wanting to do all the good things but not being concerned with his own safety, is much more disposed to fail (and, as we already know, it is in some way, the opposite of the first will). So, the situation we are discussing (the fourth) falls under

[155]

the scope of the third will (pleasant and half-hearted) as it accepts as normal the situation we are addressing: jousting with advantage over the opponent to avoid any dangers (first will) and failing due to lack of safety (second will).

In conclusion, the third will was able to please – at least partially – the first and the second wills, which is one of its major characteristics.

Therefore, to protect ourselves from the errors that are consequences of the first, second and third wills, we should act always in accordance with the fourth will, obeying to the reason and understanding: we must consider what should be done and force ourselves to do it, achieving this through effort, habit and good reason.

Let's come back to the first of the four main reasons why jousters make mistakes (mentioned earlier); knowing that everything comes from the will, we should protect ourselves from the fear of the collision, remembering everything I already wrote about it and finding the ways that we feel to be more advantageous.

I think that, if the riders have the will to joust and to succeed at the moment of collision, they would find examples and advice they could use to their advantage, if they practice them. And from all the things I said with the objective of enabling them to lose the fear of the collision, there is one that includes the understanding and the good reason and which can be used in the following way:

Throughout all the final run (from the starting of the horse's gallop at the far end of the *tea* up to the moment of collision) the jouster should keep in his mind the initial good intention to joust, not allowing it to abandon him. And the jouster should also consider the relative low level of the dangers involved in the jousts when compared with the dangers involved in doing other things such as throwing canes, hunting up and down hills and in wrestling, which are activities that most men practice without feeling fear; so, men should have the same willingness whenever they are jousting and they should also think that it is preferable to occasionally lose and fall off the horse than to miss or avoid the collision when jousting. And if they keep the necessary strong will and practice, they will not miss the collision.

Addressing now the second reason referred at the beginning of the chapter, there are three ways the jousters could use to avoid the mistakes already described:

1. The jouster should feel himself firm and at ease and carry the spear quietly and in the right direction; as soon he achieves that, he should force himself not to make any change until the collision happens.

2. A few moments before the collision, the jouster should squeeze the arm[64] against his body and keep it firm, using all his strength; if he acts as described, he will not be able to make any additional change until the collision happens.

3. Those who are not able to do as described by any of these two ways (which are the best ones) should do the following: carry the spear slightly out of the way, tense the body just at the moment of collision and simultaneously bring the spear to the collision target. This option should be used by those who know that, whenever they squeeze the arm against the body, they are unable to avoid a change of direction of the spear they are carrying; that's the reason why they cannot use anyone of the first two ways described.

---

[64] The author is, evidently, referring the arm carrying the spear.

I am going now to address the fourth reason referred at the beginning of the chapter:[65] those who, being in advantage, make mistakes. They should not overlook a careful evaluation of his opponent and the preparation of his horse and spear; only then they should joust. One point should be considered by those who know they have the advantage in a joust: they should not be afraid to carry their shields slightly below their normal position; in my opinion, those who never take chances— from time to time—are not going to become good jousters.

Besides everything I have already written, there are two additional pieces of advice that should be taken into consideration:

1. If your opponent is still a bit far away and you are already carrying your spear de soo-braço, keep it a bit lower than the point you want to hit at the collision and raise it only in the last second. This is a good advice/option for two reasons:

(1) you see your target much better and

(2) you do not allow your spear to hit your opponent below the target point you have chosen (which could happen if you carry your spear the other way around—too higher that the target point, lowering it too much at the collision).

2. The two main aspects that help you to succeed at the moment of collision are: keep your eyes on your opponent all the time and

---

[65] It looks that the author doesn't consider it possible to find corrective actions for those that are included in the third reason referred at the beginning of the chapter; and I add, almost as an afterthought, that that's why he ended that part of this chapter with this statement "...And some of them, even having the understanding of their mistakes, are unable to correct them."

[158]

maintain your body and will very strong up to the moment you see the *ruquetes*[66] of your spear hitting the target point you have chosen.

I have written so much advice about jousts that I want—in concluding this subject—to give some advice about how a jouster should take the best advantage of the men on foot that are with him. I am going to write about it because I have seen many jousters not using their men as they should (even having more than the number they need).

If a jouster has with him three men on foot and wants to use them as he should, he should have two of them at the ends of the *tea* and the other one around its middle.

The two men at the ends of the *tea* should have been given the following three responsibilities:

1. To wait for the jouster at the end of the *tea* and to guide him around it to a safe place; this is because I have seen many jousters getting wounded on their feet by the end of the *tea* (in the past, the *teas* did not have visible end marks as they currently have).

2. To take the jouster's feet out of the stirrups.

3. To keep his horse quiet.

I have another three responsibilities for the man on foot that stays around the middle of the *tea*:

1. Watch the jouster all the time and if he needs help after the collision, be quick to give it.

---

[66] *Ruquetes*—The spears used in jousts, the Portuguese way, had the pointed steel head replaced by a round flat surface with three or four embedded small spikes (the *ruquetes*); this way, the physical danger for the jousters was greatly reduced. In French and English the term was *rochets* or even *rockets*, or *coronels*, for the crown-like shape of the safety head.

2. Take care of the jouster's spear and give it to the horse's groom.

3. Watch out for any horse fittings that could have fallen down due to the collision and give them to the jouster's helpers.

One last advice for the jouster: if he has with him many men on foot, split them in three teams and give the teams the missions I have just described. This way, they will serve him much better than if they all stay around him.

Chapter XI — Teaching the rider to hunt using a spear[67], [68]

As promised I am going to give some teaching about hunting *alymarias* [wild beasts];[69] there are four ways that we may meet them:

---

[67] Once again—as in chapter V—I was forced to move a couple of paragraphs to other place within the chapter to ensure that all aspects belonging to the same subject were kept together (and not having bits and pieces belonging to the same subject all over the text); I have also introduced some additional numeric cross-references to enable the reader to easily identify where he/she was, relatively to the various subjects addressed in the chapter.

[68] Chapter XI covers the strikes that carry the spear *de soo-braço* or with both hands, while Chapter XII covers the carrying the spear *de sobre-mãao*.

[69] *Alymaria*—any wild beast (mainly big game, namely bulls and any other wild beast with horns or antlers, bears and wild pigs/boars) hunted by horse riders. During the next three chapters I will switch from the word *alymaria* to beast (or wild beast) without any special reason (to avoid writing the same word over and over again). In modern Portuguese slang, it means "a brute and stupid person" (or someone acting as such).

The Art of Riding on Every Saddle

1. The alymaria deliberately attacks us

2. We and the alymaria accidentally cross paths

3. The alymaria is running away

4. The alymaria gets caught by our dogs or comes to a stop by any other reason

I am going to describe briefly what we should do in every one of these situations in order to cause a big wound to the alymaria and also to protect ourselves from some dangerous situations and accidents that might happen due to our lack of knowledge.

1. The alymaria could deliberately attack us coming from straight ahead of us (1a), from any of our two flanks — right or left — (1b) or from behind our back (1c).

(1a) — If the alymaria comes from straight ahead of us, we should do as follows: when we are just a few moments away from the engagement[70] we use the reins (and the spurs, if required) to turn

---

[70] Collision versus engagement — I consider I have to explain my choice of these words because the author uses the word *encontro* (which is currently translated as a *meeting*) for two different situations which I name as collision and engagement.

It is also interesting to note that the author uses the word *justa* not only for a combat between two riders but also when a wild beast (an *alymaria*) attacks a rider. Actually, the *alymaria* deliberately tries to force a collision (a *justa*) whereas the rider just wants to engage, wounding the beast and avoiding a collision.

During the description of the jousts (in previous chapters) we have used many times the word collision or the term moment of collision which was considered for me as the appropriate choice for translating the original word *encontro*; the objective of the joust was, ultimately, the collision between the two jousters/ riders (we can even say that most of the previous chapters were dealing with the rules — or techniques — of collision between two jousters). In this chapter, and in the next two, I have decided

aside our horse's head to its left[71] and force it to abruptly change its direction (avoiding the collision) but in such a way that we still get very close to the shoulders of the alymaria to wound it with our spear.[72] The reason for this technique is easy to understand: if our horse and the alymaria are running against each other (in opposite directions, it is more probable we will fail to wound the beast with our spear (or not to wound it decisively) and we cannot protect ourselves if the alymaria collides with our horse.

When we are wounding the alymaria using our spear, we should choose to do it in between its shoulders (if we are facing bears, bulls and wild boars); it is the easiest place to do it because it is in the middle of its body and consequently it increases our probability of wounding the beast with our spear. If our spear wounds the alymaria around its shoulder blades we should try to hit its heart or lungs as this would result in a quicker death. And if the objective is to produce a big wound we should do the following:

---

to translate the original word *encontro* as engagement or as moment of engagement because the objective was for the rider to engage and wound the beast but to avoid the collision (so, we can also say that these next two chapters are dealing with the rules – or techniques – of engagement between a rider and an *alymaria*).

[71] It is clear for me that all the techniques to be described in the next three chapters assume right-handed riders / hunters (the reader should keep this in his/her mind when going through the descriptions). For instance, whenever a rider is chasing an 'alymaria' he does it in such a way that, when he closes in, the beast is always at his right hand side (because, being right-handed, that's where he keeps his spear).

[72] This same technique is still used today by the riders in the Portuguese bullfights, using *bandarilhas* instead of spears. Because the horse changes direction and runs faster than the bull, the rider, doing as it was just described, is able to stick the *bandarilha* on the bull's shoulder/back and to run away from it (and from the danger).

The Art of Riding on Every Saddle

If our horse is not moving fast and we are carrying our spear just slightly forward, we should—when we get to the moment of engagement—hold the spear in our hand with all our strength and wound the alymaria using all our body's weight to push the spear into its body to wound it as deeply as we can. And those who know how to do this would produce bigger and deeper wounds than others who do not know how to do it as it should be done, even if they are stronger. And to do this as it should be done, there are five pieces of advice that should be taken in consideration when we are getting to the engagement moment:

1. Turn aside the horse's head.

2. Chose very carefully the target point on the alymarias.

3. Use the body's weight to produce a big and deep wound with the spear.

4. Depending on the wound produced, withdraw the spear or not.

5. Use the spurs on the horse—as required—to avoid a collision with the alymaria (which might cause the horse to get wounded or even to fall down).

If our horse is moving fast or we are carrying our spear very much forward, we do not need to use our body's weight to push the spear into the alymarias' body; it should be enough to hold it in our hand with all our strength and the beast will suffer a big, deep wound.[73]

And we should not forget the other four points and stay very firm on the saddle (some forget that very important aspect). And if our

---

[73] Nice applied physics principles in the XVth century! Just as an example: a bullet —due to its velocity and not due to its weight—hurts a lot! That's kinetics—*the science of the relations between the motions of bodies and the forces acting upon them!*

horse is walking and if we are carrying our spear very much forward, we should not move our body to ensure that our spear hits the beast on the target point of our choice; and due to the spear's weight we need to hold it in our hand with all our strength to be able to make a big wound on the beast (which should be always possible if the spear doesn't break).

(1b)—If the alymaria comes from the right we guide our horse against it and we can wound it properly handling the spear de soo-braço.

If the alymaria comes from the left we should not handle the spear de soo-braço but with both our hands, turning our upper body to the left; nevertheless, we should avoid having our horse collide with the alymaria so, we must control it tightly and in such a way that, when we wound the beast, we can force it to go behind our horse. And those who are used to do it this way do it well and in safety.

(1c)—If the alymaria comes from behind us, the best solution is to force it to go by our left flank and, turning around our body on the saddle, wound it with our spear held in both our hands. Note that, whenever we hold the spear with both our hands, the reins are sometimes loose; it should also be noted that there are some who hold the reins in their left hand with the spear over it. In my opinion every one should do it the way he considers to be the best.

2—The alymaria comes from right to left, accidentally crossing our way, not attacking us deliberately. The best way to act is the following:

We chase the alymaria and without rushing, we get ourselves at its side, to wound it.

The alymaria comes from left to right, accidentally crossing our way, not attacking us deliberately. If we are used to wound the beast holding the spear with both our hands, we should do it. If we are only used to wound to our right, we should force our horse to a strong gallop, to get ahead of the beast and far from it; then, we should turn our horse around and be prepared to wound the beast the way we prefer. And we should make a wide turn if the alymaria is fast and a short turn if it is corpulent .

3 — The alymaria is running away

We can get to the engagement moment, in two ways:

1. We carry the spear de soo-braço and very much forward; when we get to the alymaria, we take advantage of our horse's galloping speed to strongly hit the target of our choice on the beast's body; and we should not change the positions of our body and arm to avoid any eventual change of the spear's direction.

2. We carry the spear just slightly forward, we lean our body forward and we stretch out our arm to wound the alymaria. Acting this way, we wound faster and sooner but we cannot wound so deep and decisively as in the first way just described.

These two ways are dangerous in some ways because the alymaria— when wounded—can unexpectedly turn around and attack our horse, namely its head, causing its fall and ours. There are three ways to avoid this danger:

1. When—after chasing after the alymaria—we get to it, we hit the chosen target point in the beast's body with our spear, leave it there and use the reins and the spurs if needed to get our horse away from the beast and from the danger.

2. After having caught up with the alymaria we do not wound it until we are sure we are able to do it, shall we say, in the first half of its body length. Even if the beast wants to turn around to attack our horse, our spear—which we hold strongly in our hand—makes it impossible; actually, our spear's position (and our control of it)

forces the alymaria away from us and from our horse. If we wound it near its back, it is very possible for the beast to turn around and attack our horse.

3. After having caught up with the alymaria and having wounded it, we withdraw the spear, keeping it in our hand so we can use it again if there is an attack on our horse.

In this situation, we should strongly hold the spear at the level of our horse's neck and the second wound we are able to produce in the alymaria (if our spear is a strong and resistant one) is normally decisive and the beast—even if it is a big and strong one—would immediately fall down, eventually mortally wounded.

There is another way, used by some, whenever they meet bears and wild pigs that is quite dangerous; so, you need to get specific instruction if you want to use it.

This situation happens when the alymarias run away from the place where they have their young; when they feel we are catching them, they turn back abruptly and attack our horse. It is very difficult to protect ourselves from this situation and our horse—being unexpectedly caught by the beast—could fall down.

To avoid such a disaster we should act in the following way: keeping in mind the possibility of the beast turning back abruptly and attacking our horse, we should—during the chase—keep our horse always very tightly controlled using the reins but force it to gallop very fast, trying to get ahead of the beast and put it at our right hand side; keeping the spear strongly held in our hand, we can wound it (de soo-braço or de sobre-mãao) when we are galloping at the beast's side, if we so decide.

Otherwise, we can maintain our horse's strong gallop to get well ahead of the beast and then, turn it back to face the alymaria as it should be done.

[166]

Finally, there is yet another way to wound bears, bulls and big and heavy wild boars, which I consider the safest of all:

After having chased and caught up with the alymaria we slow our horse's gallop and we go around the beast's back, getting to the other side of it; then, we increase our horse's gallop following an oblique direction towards the beast and when we get there, we wound it very strongly on its upper right hand without reducing our horse's gallop. If the alymaria turns around to attack our horse, we are already out of its immediate reach due to our speed.

4 – The alymaria gets caught by our dogs or comes to a stop for any other reason

When an alymaria is surrounded by our dogs and it is either lying down or just not moving, the normal option taken by many is to wound it de sobre-mãao; nevertheless, those who want to wound properly in this situation should carry the spear slightly forward and strike using the help of their body's weight. Doing it this way, they wound with more accuracy and it is easier to move the horse around ensuring better protection for their dogs.

My father – my king and my lord – gives some advice about these subjects (namely about how to wound quicker) in his *Livro da Montaria* [Book of big game hunting]; as examples of his advice, I mention two points: we should not frequently carry the spear de soo-braço (to avoid miss hitting the target) and we should drive the alymarias through narrow ways or to foothills (making it impossible for them to turn around unexpectedly to attack our horse).

Chapter XII — Teaching the rider to wound, carrying the spear de sobre-mãao[74]

To wound properly carrying the spear de sobre-mãao, there are the following points to be taken into consideration:

First of all, we should consider if we are facing (1) wild beasts with strong defenses — horns, antlers or tusks — or (2) wild beasts without them (who are much easier to wound with the spear).

1. You should hold the spear strongly in your hand, keeping your arm loose and staying as much at ease as possible, strike with your spear using all your strength. In this situation you cannot get any additional advantage from your body's weight to wound deeper

---

[74] Don't forget that, in accordance with the chapter's title, in all the techniques described in this chapter, the rider carries the spear *de sobre-mãao* (otherwise this chapter could have been considered almost just as a repetition of parts of chapter XI).
I find it useful and appropriate to remember the reader the two techniques the riders use to carry the spear in their hands:
de sobre-mãao — the spear is held horizontally, resting over the forearm
de soo-braço — the spear is held obliquely, supported at the armpit The reader should perhaps imagine he is in the rider's shoes and try to reproduce his body's movements, in accordance with the descriptions given.
It is also important to note that the author used in the earlier chapters the words beast and horse as synonyms (because the only animal included in his writings were horses). Since he started to address hunting activities (because there were other animals involved, like bulls, boars, animals with antlers, etc.) horse and beast ceased to be considered as synonyms; a horse was a horse and a beast was a beast (horse excluded). He also introduced the word 'alymaria' as a synonym of a wild beast hunted by riders.

because you might be in a difficult situation due to the wild beast's defenses.

2. Not having the danger represented by the wild beast's defenses, you should raise your arm and elbow high, hold the spear strongly in your hand and tight to your body. At the moment of wounding you should stretch your arm and use all the advantage you can get from your body's weight to push forward your spear. Doing it in this way, there are four forces used in the strike:

1st — From the horse's gallop

2nd — From the movement of your arm

3rd — From your body's weight

4th — From your hand

And those who know how to do these techniques well will be able — if the target point on the beast is well chosen and the spear is a good one — to pierce with the spear right through the bodies of bears, bulls and boars, if the spear doesn't hit the beast's bones on its way through their bodies.

And they should have as objective to really pierce through the beast's body completely, to see the steel's sharp head of the spear on the other side of the beast's body, because if they are happy just for having hurt the beast — not wounding it with the objective of having the spear going through from one side of its body to the other — they wound worse than those who have that objective and in order to achieve it, they go on pushing the spear forward with their arms and bodies weight until the spear no longer penetrates the beast's body.

And those who are good horsemen, who ride and hunt at ease without making errors, do it with such apparent simplicity that

[169]

others who do not know them well are unable to correctly evaluate their skills.

And all these descriptions should be considered as generic advice on wounding, carrying the spear de sobre-mãao. Here are some additional details: the horse riders who are hunting, might find game either because (1), they are attacked by it, (2) they see the wild beast running away or (3) it is surrounded by the dogs.

1. If the beast is jousting the best way to act is the following:

keep your hand quiet and firm at the level of your face, your elbow high and wait for the beast; if your position is correct, the beast will probably impale itself on your spear; then, it is the time for you to use all your body's weight to push your spear forward, penetrating deeply into the beast's body (as if you were carrying the spear de soobraço).

In this situation—the beast is attacking you—this is the best technique to wound it, when you are carrying the spear de sobre-mãao. If you raise your arm only when the beast is very close to you, you might not have enough time to put the spear in the correct position and you might miss the engagement moment because the beast, having not stopped running, is already out of reach.

2. If the beast is running away and you want to wound it faster and sooner you do not need to get at its side; when you get near the beast, lean your body forward and stretch your arm to wound it (keeping the spear strongly held in your hand). It happens many times that the beast stops and makes a move against the direction of the spear (already deep in its body) causing itself an even greater wound. But this wounding technique is dangerous as the beast can, unexpectedly, turn around and attack your horse (namely its head or its chest); if this happens, due to the fact that the rider's body is leaning forward and he has no time to use the reins to control the

horse, he might fall down over the horse's head. Therefore, in order to produce the biggest possible wound on the beast and to stay safely mounted, it is better for the rider not to act in haste; he should wait until he gets at the beast's side to wound it with the spear, without leaning his body forward.

3. If the beast is surrounded by dogs, the rider should wound the beast with the spear, keeping his arm squeezed against his upper body and not raising it too much; the rider should also keep a good and tight control of the horse's bridle and should not stop his horse to wound the beast. If he does that, the spear's strike will happen later than if the horse was still moving towards the beast and he will produce a weaker wound. Those who know how to do this technique well (with two or three dogs around the beast) do it at ease and safely; even if the beast is not completely stopped and is moving around the dogs, the riders—keeping tight control of the horse's bridle—are able to use their body's weight to help the arm to produce a deep wound. To throw down to the ground an alymaria I use a specific technique I have found through my own experience and for which I need to be carrying a strong and long spear: immediately after having produced a deep wound in the alymaria, I push the spear with a sudden push ground wards. Few beasts are not immediately thrown to the ground; nevertheless, many spears are broken using this technique.

When the dogs find a wild boar we should see whether the beast keeps running forward or whether it starts moving around the dogs; if it is running forward, the rider should run after it as fast as he can and wound it with the spear; if it is moving around the dogs, the rider should pay attention to its movements and strike with the spear only when he is sure of wounding it. Whatever the situation, the hunter should not forget that it is always preferable to wound a beast with the horse in movement than after it has stopped; it is better and the rider shows himself to be at ease. And all these

[171]

hunting techniques are very useful in combat because a skilled hunter strikes well with the spear, causing deeper wounds on the enemy's body. I found through my own experience that—when hunting—we should carry big and heavy spears, even considering that those who carry lighter ones are more agile.

But I can say that I am the one who carries the biggest and heaviest spears of all those who normally hunt with me and I do not find, among them all, anyone that I consider to have any advantage over me just because he is carrying a lighter spear.

And I praise myself as a hunter because I believe I am an example that should be followed by others; it is my understanding that if we believe we are saying the truth and in accordance with the reason, we can praise ourselves, and do not deserve to be censured because of it.[75]

Chapter XIII — Teaching the rider how to throw the spear

There are four things necessary to those who want to throw the spear well:

First, to throw far

Second, to hit the target

Third, to throw safely, protecting himself and the horse from accidents with the spear, and

Fourth, to throw with elegance

---

[75] Amazing statements from D. Duarte! He is normally so humble! He must have been a hunting fanatic.

First, to throw far: those who want to do it well, with the spear reaching great distances, should start practicing on foot, using spears identical to the ones they will use when mounted, with the objective of getting used to the correct movement of the arm. those who do not practice on foot should not expect to be able to do well when riding.

To throw the spear on foot, some run with the spear held in a low position, others with it in a high position, throwing it from there. The best technique to throw the spear when riding, looks to be throwing it from a high position. Unfortunately I was unable to get used to it; I carry the spear high but when I want to throw it, I lower my arm and throw the spear immediately; I consider both techniques correct. But you should never have the arm already stretched in a high position at the start of the horse's run or delay the spear's throw after you lower your arm; both of them are ineffective techniques.

In order for riders to be able to throw the spear at great distances they should, for safety reasons, start practicing using pointless shafts. With the horse already at a steady gallop they should move the arm as they were doing it when practicing on foot and throw the spear into the air from an initial high position with a sudden movement of the arm[76], using all their strength; with the additional force that comes from the horse's speed, the spear reaches much greater distances than what the rider initially expected[77].

---

[76] Or one might say "with a jerk."

[77] The movement of the arm to throw the spear is identical to the one done nowadays by the javelin throwers in athletics (as the author will mention later on during this chapter).

[173]

The rider should go on practicing until he is sure he has acquired all the required skills to throw the spear well, especially the sudden movement of the arm, which only few are able to master. The rider should also learn to correctly evaluate the consequences of the additional weight of the spear's head and hold it in his hand at the correct point, ensuring that, when he throws the spear into the air it goes on in the direction intended by the thrower. After having practiced for several days at gallop and being sure that he already knows how the spears throw should be done, the rider should start practicing other throwing techniques because this art is the art that a rider should practice more than any other. When the rider is practicing on foot, he should never use shafts that are too heavy or too light, because — as a consequence of the sudden movement of his arm throwing an unusual weight in the air — he can sprain or dislocate it; while if he is riding and throws a spear with the weight he is used to, he will never hurt his arm — unless it is already ailing. And if the rider throws the spear well when mounted, he will not get any additional advantage by practicing on foot with spears too heavy or too light, as I have already learned through my own experience.

If a rider wants to throw a spear very far, he should be riding a horse with a Gineta saddle and short stirrups straps, carrying the spear as he is accustomed to and with the arm relaxed and loose; then, he gets his horse on a steady gallop, through flat ground, with the wind coming from behind and not touching the horse's bridle until he throws the spear (having also in mind all my advice). Doing it this way, he should be able to throw the spear exceeding at least by one-third the distance he normally reaches when he throws it on foot. I have tested it myself and I was able to throw the spear to a distance of sixteen times its length (as against eleven times its length which was the distance I was able to get when running on foot and wearing an appropriate doublet). I mention this specific example to enable each one to evaluate his own skills, comparing the distances he can throw his spear when on a steady gallop and when running on foot. And I strongly advise the riders not to try other techniques with the objective of throwing spears farther; for example, if they stop the horse at the moment they throw, they will get very negative results. Also, they should not use the spurs frequently during the horse's gallop: they should allow the horse to get on a steady gallop and then use the spurs just once — the horse immediately increases the pace of its gallop and that is the proper moment for you to throw the spear[78].

Second, to hit the target: First of all it should be considered whether the target is nearby. If it is a deer that it is far away from you and moving, you have to estimate where the deer will be when it can be hit by your spear; once you have done that, you should throw your spear not directly at the deer's current position but at the position you have calculated; and you will hit or not depending on practice and luck.

If the deer is nearby — and right in front of you — you should never throw your spear to a point straight ahead because it is dangerous and it increases the probability of missing the target; you should keep the spear in your hand, chose a target on the deer's body (its shoulder is a good one) and throw the spear with a sudden movement of your arm as if you were throwing a javelin. Do not forget that, to hit your target is much more important than the strength you use to throw the spear; this is due to the fact that your horse's speed helps the spear to cause a deep wound — even if it is thrown without too much strength. And if you throw the spear

---

[78] The horse's acceleration produces an additional force that is added to the energy the rider spends to throw the spear. The same will be noted in making the sword more effective to wound from horseback.

when your horse is not moving—as it happens many times with hunters who are very close to the target—do it as if you were throwing a javelin, which is a game I have found to be very useful in training a man in the throwing of spears and successfully hitting the chosen targets, wherever he is on foot or mounted.

Third, to throw safely: In order to ensure you throw a spear safely, there are only two instructions you have to follow:

1. Never throw a spear to a point straight ahead of you.

2. After you have thrown a spear turn your horse to a direction opposite to the one you have thrown the spear.

Fourth, to throw with elegance: To throw the spear with elegance you have to pay attention to three things:

First, have the appropriate horse, saddle, clothes and spear. *Second*, keep your feet, legs and body correctly placed, consider the arm which is carrying the spear your main lever and stay quiet in the saddle at the throwing moment, and *Third*, having in mind all the advice already given, throw an appropriate spear with all your strength. The heavy spears require you to have your arm and shoulder loose and relaxed at the throwing moment. The light spears and the canes require you to throw the spear with a sudden movement centered in the middle of your arm.

I have to say that—when I was riding—I threw many spears (and hit the target) against bears, boars and deer; but I have also failed many times due to several factors such as the beast's movements, my position on the saddle, the wind, the uneven ground, the wrong choice of the point to handle the spear, its weight, or being too hasty and not having prepared the throw as I should have; therefore, do not consider it odd whenever your spear misses the beast because there are many factors that can cause just that.

[176]

And, as far as this art of throwing the spear is concerned do not forget that it is worth to practice it and to acquire the skills needed to master it even if — for obvious reasons — it is of no importance to those who wear a *braçal*[79].

It is an art very useful in many situations namely hunting, playing with canes and doing other things that are usually done by good men, either mounted or on foot.

Chapter XIV — *Teaching the rider how to wound using a sword*

As far as advice for a rider to wound effectively using a sword are concerned, there are in my opinion four main ways to do it:

First, to wound with the cutting-edge of the sword, performing a horizontal rotation with the arm that holds it.

Second, to wound with the cutting-edge of the sword, performing an oblique rotation with the arm that holds it.

Third, to wound with the cutting-edge of the sword, performing a vertical top-down movement with the arm that holds it.

Fourth, to wound with a thrust of the tip of the sword.

The first two are — in my opinion — the best ways to wound another rider; and to cause great wounds with a horizontal rotation of the arm that holds the sword, you should use the combined forces of the horse's gallop, of your upper body and of your arm, all together.

---

[79] Protective armor for the arm.

This was the solution I have found more efficient in tournaments[80]; if the horse was not at gallop and I used only the force of my arm, the stroke was much weaker than if I could use the three forces simultaneously.

This is now an advice for all those who want to make perfect, harmonious and beautiful strokes with a sword: when you are coming back against your adversaries (assuming you have passed through them the first time without being forced into or attempting any collision or engagement), you firm your legs on the saddle, you keep your upper body and the arm holding the sword loose and relaxed with the sword strongly held in your hand and you do your stroke with an oblique top-down rotation of the arm that holds the sword. And to have time to prepare yourself, you should not make (in important tournaments, with many riders) short turns with your horse and you should also not choose in advance any specific adversary, unless you are sure to be in great advantage over him (like for example, if he has his back to you).

---

[80] It is clear that the author is describing the best tactics that should be used in tournaments (and certainly in combats) between two teams of riders (and they look to have been quite bloody).
I consider extraordinary the detailed description of his strategy and tactic as he is giving away (to his adversaries / enemies) a most valuable advantage he has over them and that might actually represent the difference between to be a winner or a loser (eventually seriously wounded or even dead).
It is one thing is to do that type of teaching about jousts; it may be quite another one to do it for use in tournaments and combats with swords in which the objective is really to wound the adversary!
When D. Duarte wrote this chapter, either he was already King of Portugal or the Crown Prince. So, he could not allow himself to participate in such dangerous events. He could teach all his readers but he could not put his life and his Kingdom's future in jeopardy.

If you have a brave horse that reacts correctly to the spurs, which is not easily frightened[81]48 and which is well prepared with good harness, you should go through to the end of the tournament field and take care in turning your horse around, because I have already seen many fall down doing just that.

Returning to the tournament field, you should wound with no hesitation the first adversary you find on your way and go on looking for any other—but without turning your horse around—until you get to the other end of the tournament field. Then, turning your horse back to return to the action, you have time to see what's going on; if you see some of your friends surrounded by adversaries and fighting vigorously, you should gallop through the attack—destroying it with your action—and keep on galloping through the field, eventually finding another adversary to wound.

Acting as described you gets the following advantages:

1. Your performance is easily noticed by the audience.

2. Your strokes are stronger because you wound whom you decide and you will find many adversaries you can wound with no difficulty or danger for you.

3. Your horse stays strong because you do not tire it with successive and abrupt changes of direction; rather, you keep it at a steady gallop for most of the action.

Acting as I said, your strokes are at intervals and you do not tire your arm, which is not the case with many others. As I have found through my experience what I have just described should be used by those who want to enjoy the advantages I have also referred to.

---

[81] Skittish.

And if you need to wound fast with a stroke of your sword (and time might be a decisive factor in the situation you are facing) you should just use an oblique rotation of the arm that holds the sword, not spending any time to prepare for the simultaneous rotation of your upper body in order to ensure a more decisive wound.

The third stroke (a top-down movement of the arm holding the sword) is rarely used against other riders but it is advisable against adversaries on foot or against alymarias; you should hold the sword strongly in your hand and transfer all the strength of your body to the stroke in order to cause a great wound; in this technique — the transfer of the strength of your body to the stroke in the top-down movement of your arm holding the sword — it is very important to avoid wounding your foot or your horse with the sword.

And remembering what I said about the importance of the habit of learning all arts, those who want to learn this art must practice it frequently, which is the only way not to forget it; if you master it, you will find yourself at an advantage in many specific situations.

One final advice to those who want to keep their arms in good physical condition (which is also important for the throwing of the spear): you should not play peella[82] or throwing things too light or too heavy as it might only cause damage to your arm and it doesn't bring any benefit.

The fourth option is to wound with a thrust of the sword's tip.

The technique is similar to the one described to wound with the spearde sobre-mãao:

---

[82] See glossary.

Holding the weapon in your hand (horizontally) and pushing forward with your body. You can wound an alymaria keeping your sword pointing to the outside (relatively to your horse) to avoid having the alymaria—after it is wounded—attack your horse's head; the safest way is to cause a deep wound in the alymaria with the sword (using your body's weight to push forward your sword's tip into the alymarias body).

And I have written in detail about these arts for all the reasons I have already mentioned and for the benefits that some could get from this advice, because I do believe that they are some of the principles that enable the good horsemen to be at their ease.

As time goes by, the habits, the customs and the arts of the various regions change and it is possible that, in some places, precisely the contrary of what I wrote might be considered appropriate; nevertheless, everybody should understand that I have written what I wrote based on my own experience, which is in accordance with what it is currently considered the good practice in the kingdom of our King, my lord and my father, whose soul is under God[83].

And I say this, not to praise myself, even considering that any man is allowed to say whatever he finds correct about these arts; I do it to transmit authority to what I wrote and to give value to its reading, because I did it, not just having heard about it but because I learned it through long practice and great experience.

And to the lords I give one advice that—if followed—would enable them to show that they are at ease and also to get some benefits out of it:

---

[83] It is evident that this chapter was written after the death of D. Duarte's father, King D. João I, in 1433.

They should practice jumping from the ground to the horse's saddle without having any helper to take care of the reins or of the stirrups; they should practice it, helping themselves either with the right or left hand and sometimes even carrying a spear in one of the hands and a hunting bird (an hawk, for example) over their right foot; they should start practicing it with small horses and then with bigger ones; and they should keep on practicing even if they are not wearing appropriate clothes; if they do it frequently, they will be able to do it reasonable well, even if they are strongly built. Finally, they should also practice it, wearing their full body armor.

It is written in the *Livro do Regimento dos Principes* [*De Regimine Principum*] whose author was Giles of Rome[84] that the Roman riders — when they were not at war — kept practicing inside their homes; they had wooden horses and their practice included the proper preparation and fixing of the whole harness and saddle and the training for the jumps that I have just described. And they considered this practise to be very useful.

Speaking about my own experience, there were times when I practiced those jumping exercises regardless of the size of the horse and of the clothes I was wearing. And when I lost that habit I considered that I had lost something valuable.

So, I advise the lords to go on practicing that habit as I am sure they will take benefits out of it. And I remember my King — my lord and my father — (to be glorified by God) as a good example of this practice: because he did it since he was very young, when he was over seventy years old he still did it showing an agility and easiness difficult to be matched by men fifty years old.

---

[84] Also known as *Frei Gil de Roma*.

What I have seen done by him and by others like him and what I feel from my own experience is more than enough to justify my advice, which I believe will be beneficial to all those who decide to keep that habit.

Chapter XV—Praises for the personal skills and virtues

I have been written in great detail about the various arts practiced when riding, for two reasons: I am accustomed to writing and I have a great affection for all these arts.

I recollect various arts that require strength, quickness, deftness and strong arms that were very much practiced by our knights and squires and which are nowadays almost forgotten—much to my displeasure and sadness. All my statements, advice and teaching have not been enough to stimulate and renew their practice.

And many times, those who were forced to test the level of their current skills did it in such a way which in no way pleased me, having in mind the expertise I remember existing in the past, in my household.

All this happens due to the lack of will to keep and develop those skills; this situation is, in my opinion, due to the fact that most men are currently so much influenced by the women that they have started favoring other things such as wearing smart and elegant clothes and shoes, playing *peella*, singing and dancing just to please them, ceasing to practice the arts they once mastered[85].

---

[85] However, it is considered by Portuguese historians that the power and importance achieved by King D. João I (Father of D. Duarte) during his

Considering that the will is the most important factors influencing the human behavior, if it diminishes in regard to certain activities, those activities are not learned anymore — as they were before — and are easily forgotten.

I think that the current situation is the consequence of the times and the world's evolution everywhere — not only in our Kingdom — and the fundamental reasons for it are not easy to identify.

One thing I can say relatively to my house:

All the specific activities practiced by me were also practiced by all those who were close to me and by all the others. But, when — due to my great responsibilities — I was forced to reduce or cease the practice of some arts, those who were close to me did the same and were followed by all the others, because the examples coming from the top are always followed , even in those things which concern their way of life, by those around them. This is the reason why the knights and the squires who are under the protection of the most important lords, go on practicing some specific arts when — due to that practice — they are praised by them; and all the others do the same. At the contrary, if the most important ones do not practice a specific art, it should not be expected that that art will continue to be practiced by the others with the necessary expertise.

As a conclusion, the example of the most important personalities are followed by all the others in the house or in the kingdom.

A similar situation occurs concerning the practicing of the virtues; I am pleased to see that currently — thanks to God and also due to the

---

reign were very much enhanced by the great level of education, virtuosity, personality and influence of his wife D. Phillipa de Lancaster, granddaughter of King Edward III of England.

good examples—the kindness and other virtues that have always been seen in our King,—my lord and my father, and by our virtuous Queen, my lady and my mother, were followed by the most important personalities of our Kingdom (and, in general, by everybody else); it is a fact that there were great improvements in the virtues and a great reduction in the practice of bad habits.

In the same way I feel sad due to the general reduction in the physical skills, I also have to recognize and praise—thanks be to God—the improvement in the practice of virtues and in the abandonment of bad habits.

Nevertheless, the practice of the virtues should not have had any influence in the reduction of the practice and development of physical activities, because they were always highly considered and praised by all, which could be seen in the book *De Re Militari* from Flavius Vegetius Renatus[86], and in other books of histories and instruction in deeds of war.

And even considering that the physical activities/arts that currently are more commonly practiced are good ones, it should not be forgotten that the arts that are the most important for combat, are the ones that we should—above all others—learn and master.

Therefore I advise all the lords and youths to consider their bodies as if they were their estates; if they are not taken care of—properly cultivated—they will yield nothing but cardoons, thorns and herbs of small or no value; nevertheless, with the correct work, they will yield fruits so important that we can benefit from them throughout all our lives.

---

[86] An influential treatise about military arts, written around the end of the century IV A.D.

And if during our youth we did not exercise our bodies – leaving them in total idleness – they will progressively become worthless and will deserve to be given to others *de sesmaria*[87], to be forced to work as servants and to perform activities appropriate to their capabilities; in this way, they will not consume the provisions that should be given only to the good workers.

To avoid such errors, all youths of good lineage – if they are brought up in homes where this becomes possible – should be taught to read, to write and to speak Latin and to follow on their education with the reading of good books which might guide them to virtuous lives.

There are some who say that those readings are not appropriate for persons of such high status; the fact is that we must believe we have a soul and so, we all should work – with our God's help – to its salvation; and I say that we can achieve that – under God – through the study of good books and good conversation. We should read the good philosophy books that cover the moral subjects and which teach – in many different ways – the good customs and the practice of the virtues; we should also be taught about all the things referred in those books and we should have the will to practice them.

We should also read the books that cover the arts of war because their chronicles and narratives are very important reading, making us aware of great deeds and good examples; doing this, the lords, knights and their sons would then be able to learn from them the wisdom and the knowledge that could help them very much – under God – in times of need.

All the skills that require physical activity from the body- to be performed in accordance with its status – should never be

---

[87] See glossary.

disregarded, especially riding and wrestling, as they are the most important ones and through them it is possible to achieve great honor; if the riding skills represent a great help and advantage to all the arts performed on a horse, wrestling keeps those who are accustomed to walk on foot unafraid of doing so.

And wrestling keeps our body in good shape, which is of the utmost importance for war and for all other good physical activities. And if during our youth those skills were not properly practiced and taught, it is still possible to achieve reasonable levels when we are older.

And the noblemen who practice these arts (improving and maintaining their physical skills) in the lords' households, are able to chase away boredom from those who live there, simultaneously increasing their reputation and making them more feared by others, assuming they keep the necessary kindness and other virtues.

And those lords should be praised and rewarded more than others who do otherwise, who do not develop those skills; and all these activities should be practiced as recreation and entertainment by all the servants of the lords and all those who visit them as it is the case of the noblemen who are there practicing their physical skills.

Chapter XVI—A brief description of the wrestling techniques[88]

For specific reasons—to be mentioned later in this chapter—I have ordered to be briefly written a description of the most important techniques used in wrestling; nevertheless, those who become really interested in learning them should ask for lessons from any good teacher of wrestling, because nobody becomes skilled in this art just from reading what it is written about it.

---

[88] Without taking in consideration any eventual differences between the current rules of wrestling and the rules of that fighting art in the XVth century in Portugal, I have decided to use the word wrestling, which I have already mentioned near the end of the last chapter, as the translation for *luyta* the word
used by D. Duarte for that fighting art, and which is etymologically related to the modern *lutte*, a term for an obscure, traditional grappling art practiced in various forms in France.
As I do not consider myself skilled enough in any style of wrestling to accurately analyze what is described herein, I was forced to ask a friend to help me out, translating into the current Portuguese language the more than twenty wrestling techniques that are described in this chapter (following D. Duarte's example, who ordered a qualified professor to describe them). So, I have to thank Mr. Paulo Martins, a University Professor of wrestling, and a former Portuguese Olympic athlete, for his most valuable cooperation; I would not have overcome this difficulty without his help. After that done, my son Luis Franco Preto (who holds a Master of Sciences degree in Physical Education) translated it into the English language. I then sent it to my publisher, who in turn then had Mr.Roger Siggs, of Phoenix, AZ, who has nearly three decades of experience in aikido, jujutsu and wrestling, and currently researches and teaches medieval European wrestling, review the description of the techniques, and compare them to other medieval treatises. Hopefully, between all of our efforts, we have faithfully conveyed the meaning Dom Duarte's instructions to a modern, English language, audience.

The techniques that are going to be described—over twenty of them— are techniques I have practiced and also some others that I have seen used by some good wrestlers (no wrestler used all of them, but only those he liked most)[89].

---

[89] Wrestling has a pedigree in the West that extends back to the ancient Greeks. D. Duarte's twenty techniques of wresting are quite interesting because they represent a style of sportive wrestling, not dissimilar from modern, upright, free-style wrestling. Other early European wrestling sources (all from Germany
and northern Italy) also focus on "stand-up" wrestling, but with a particular emphasis on lethal grappling, best suited for the battlefield. Techniques emphasize throws, arm bars, neck and joint-locks, breaks and unarmed defenses against a weapon; often applied following an initial percussive strike to the face, throat, chest, or floating ribs, with the goal of quickly incapacitating
the opponent, perhaps to immediately face another. However, one of the earliest texts to present such, *Il Fior di Battaglia* ("The Flower of Battle" – 1409), composed by the Italian master-at-arms, Fiore dei Liberi da Premariacco, makes it clear that a more sportive type of wrestling was also commonly practiced:
Let us begin now with wrestling, which can be of two sorts: from pleasure; or from anger, that is, for preserving life, and using every manner of deceit, falsity and cruelty that is possible. I wish to speak of that which is made for life and to reveal it through its principles, and especially to show how to gain the holds that are used when fighting for your life.
(Il Fior di Battaglia: MS Ludwig XV 13—J. Paul Getty Museum, folio 3v.)

A generation or so after dei Liberi, the German wrestling master Ott taught both disciplines, and the extensive corpus of his techniques, which survives through the written and illustrated works of his disciples, taught a number of hugs and takedowns, as well as a number of ground fighting and submission techniques. (For examples of the German tradition, see the "von Danzig Fechtbuch," c.1452, Cod.44A8, Biblioteca Nazionale, Rome, Hans Talhoffer's 1467 *Fechtbuch* Cod.icon.394a, Bayerische Staatsbibliothek München, reprinted in Mark Rector (trans.), *Medieval Combat*, Greenhill Press, 2000, Hans Wurm, *Ringerbuch* c.1492, or the anonymous "Codex Wallerstein, Cod.I.6.40.2 Augsburgbibliothek, reprinted and translated in Grzegorz Zabinski, The *Codex Wallerstein: A Medieval Fighting Book from the Fifteenth Century on the Longsword, Falchion, Dagger, and Wrestling*, Paladin

The "Hook" in an anterior takedown[90] with an inside control of the arm with an inward hook, meaning that, from the base position of vertical wrestling,[91] the attacker, controlling the head with one and one arm with the other, executes a hooking action to the defender's forward leg, and continues the movement by accompanying the fall of the defender.

He finalizes with a control of the waist and arm.[92]

Other forms of the "Takedown with a Hook" can be executed in five ways, from what is known:

1. Controlling and arm by the inside with both hands;

Press, 2002). In the 16th and 17th centuries, as wrestling continued to develop into a form of sportive physical exercise the strikes, throws and joint-breaks increasingly gave way in favor of the relatively safer takedowns, chokes and pins.

[90] (It is understood, based on the chapter's first paragraph, that all the technical descriptions that follow were not written by D. Duarte).
A *take-down* means putting the opponent on the floor without having him becoming airborne (always remaining in contact with the floor).

[91] Basic "stand up position" — the wrestler is standing up. The legs and arms are flexed, separated by the shoulders width, with one leg slightly forward and the arms directed forward, in a position facing the opponent from the front. Thanks to Mr. Paulo Martins for his specific assistance on this point.

[92] This is a single leg hook, a common wrestling "take down," but the initial description is unclear as to whether the upper body is moved in one direction and the lower in another, or more like catch wrestling where it's a forward drive. Variants of both actions are represented in 15th century German and Italian sources, and survive in modern styles of folk wrestling, today.

2. Performing the hook without any previous control in a fast and energetic action, by finalizing with a control of the attacker's neck;

3. Performing a control of the neck with both hands in order to, right away and quickly, apply the hook to one leg;

4. Performing a reverse body lock, in which both arms are controlled from above;

5. Controlling the neck with both hands, pulling him energetically underneath very quickly and applying the hook to the leg.

The "Hook with a Trip" is also an anterior take down with an inside control of the arm with an interior hook, meaning that from the base position of vertical wrestling, the attacker, controlling the head with one hand and one arm with another hand, executes a hook to the defender's forward leg, this time sliding the leg and elevating the hook.

He continues the movement by accompanying the fall of the defender, and finalizes with the control of the waist and arm.

Also the "Hooks with a Turn of the Hip" are performed this same way, with the difference of turning the hip according to the direction of the trip, which can be forward, backwards or to the side where the action over the neck is tighter.

The throws[93] used with hooks to the legs can be performed in three different ways: from the base wrestling position, the opponent is

---

[93] Modern kinesthologists have replaced "throw" with *projection*, which means putting the opponent on the ground having him momentarily loose contact with the ground (becoming airborne), as against "*take downs*." in which the opponent doesn't become airborne. Because "projection" is technical and not yet in wide use, I have preferred to stay with "throw."

controlled by grabbing both his legs and applying the hook to the interior heel, in the exterior or to the opposite heel.[94]

Another type of throw is performed putting the opponent into the ground on his back, and it can be done in six different ways:

1. From a standing position one controls the waist and the arms close to the body and turns the opponent to the ground.

2. Another one is identical but without controlling the arms.

3. From a standing position one controls the waist, gets up and turns the fighter to the ground.

4. From a standing position one controls the waist, gets up arching the back and turns the fighter to the ground.

5. From a standing position one controls the waist and the arms close to the body, gets up arching the back and turns the fighter to the ground, by first faking to one side and then executing to the other side

6. From a standing position one controls the waist and the head, turning the fighter to the ground.[95]

We can also take down or project with a reverse body lock in three different ways:

1. From a standing position one controls the waist with a reverse body lock, gets ups and turns the fighter to the ground;

---

[94] A trip.

[95] This is hug wrestling, utilizing a variety of body locks and lifts still common today.

2. From a standing position one controls the waist and the arms close to the body with a reverse body lock, gets ups and turns the fighter to the ground;

3. Controlling the neck with a reverse body lock can also perform it[96].

It is also possible to project the opponent sideways, using one's own back: In a standing position or with one knee on the ground, one controls the opponent, grabbing one arm and putting his own back under the opponent, getting himself up and pulling, making the opponent to pass over him on his way to the ground.

It can also be performed by controlling the opponent's arm and his waist and, in the same way, putting our back under the opponent, getting up and pulling, making him pass or go over and in the direction of the arm.

Finally, it can also be done by controlling the opponent's arm and the waist and, in the same way, putting our back under the opponent, getting up and pulling, making him pass or go over and in the direction of the arm, but simultaneously turning the opponent in the air, projecting him in a reverse way or in the opposite direction.

The take down to the front can be performed by controlling both arms from the outside,[97] and the force is applied in the direction of the leg that is farther away[98].

---

[96] The control is attained by capturing the opponent in a headlock under the wrestler's armpit.

[97] Which is nowadays known as "control of the arms from above."

Another wrestling technique, and consisting of a forward take down can be performed by controlling both arms from the outside, applying the force in the direction of the leg which is farthest away (pushing him) using a hook.

The forward take down can also be done by controlling both arms from the outside, applying the force in the direction of the chest and transporting him to the ground.

One can also make a take down in the same way, but by controlling one arm with one hand and grabbing the opponent's neck with the other.

Controlling the feet with the hands and near the heels, always pushing until the fighter falls, can also attain taking the opponent down.

Chest-to-chest take downs can be performed in two ways:

1. Facing the opponent from the front one fakes an entry to the neck and, when he lifts his arms, they are both controlled and the take down is performed.

2. One gets in first with one arm to the opponent's back and next, without releasing, gets inside, closing both hands in back and pushing.

---

[98] The leg of the opponent being thrown; not the leg of the person applying the throw.

The passages to the back can be performed in three ways:

1. Controlling[99] one of the opponent's hands, one swings himself and jumps backwards.

2. One can grab both opponent's hands, pull them downwards and jump himself backwards, always maintaining a grip on at least one of the opponent's hands.

3. The last one is done pulling the opponent's neck down and then sliding himself back.

There are three different ways to take down the opponent backwards:

First, both arms are elevated, and controlled until reaching the ground.

The *second* way is reached using the same way of controlling the arms but turning the opponent around. Releasing one of the arms, the fighter is pulled to the ground.

The *third*: from the double control of the arms one foot is placed near the companion's foot, tripping him and thus taking him down forward.

To use the chest, one needs to lift the opponent and move one foot or another forward and perform the technique to the side.

Also, when the neck is grabbed turning the shoulders and crossing with one hand or the arm the other's throat, and quickly performs a trip with the foot, changing control to the arms.

---

[99] Grabbing.

There is also a technique[100] when one controls the arm and the head and, turning the hip, one lowers himself to a kneeling position, until taking the other one to the ground is also good. One should tighten the neck really well so that the other one doesn't escape with his head, which usually happens.

When the fighters are involved in fights outside their own properties, they are usually dressed and so it is possible to have fights when still wearing clothes and thus, by grabbing the shirt at shoulder level, one is able to immobilize the arms so as to pass over with one arm and charge him with the chest in the direction of the ground[101].

Or if we wish to play a risky game, but one which can give us great advantage, we go over the opponent's arm with one of our arms, controlling it by just the hand of the opponent; then, we twist it in the elbow area and in the hand and you'll see that, little by little, they will kneel to the floor due to the intense pain that this produces. However, it is necessary to notice that this technique may break his arm or dislocate the hand if not conveniently performed, which therefore should restrict its use in friendly fights[102].

Nobody should think that this art is not proper to be practiced by the most important personalities of State, landlords and noblemen; my King—my Lord and my Father—whose soul is with God—

---

[100] Although seldom or rarely used in modern wrestling, this is quite common in Asian grappling arts such as aikido or jujutsu.

[101] A basic technique of jacket wrestling, which, while little practiced in the Western world today, is the foundation of Japanese judo or Russian sambo.

[102] A variant of a forearm throw. Again, notice the emphasis on sportive wrestling. We understand that, from this point onwards, is again D. Duarte's writing.

practiced this art frequently and was a very good wrestler; and the princes and captains mastered so well this art that there were not many others able to match their skills. And in my Court, when I still practiced it, there were so many good wrestlers that I also think that their skills were not easily matched by others[103].

Unfortunately many do not currently practice this art and I feel sorrow for it because I would have liked to see its popularity back. But, I think that, due to certain known reasons[104] and other unpleasant situations, that is not going to happen; but, considering that new things do not exist only in heaven and that it is always possible for an old thing to be considered again as a new thing, I hope that—still in my life time— wrestling becomes again a fashionable art.

And besides all the wrestling techniques already referred, there are other techniques used by some to throw their opponents to the ground; and each one uses his own specific skills to neutralize the opponent's attacks and their effectiveness are a direct consequence of their knowledge and the frequency of their practice of this art. And I write this with the objective of convincing some to learn— sooner or later—this art (which would not happen if they do not read my writings).

I have decided to include this chapter about wrestling in my book about horse riding, understanding that it does not look to belong to

---

[103] D.Duarte echoes the importance placed on wrestling as a foundation of martial endeavor by dei Liberi (1409) and Pietro Monte, *De dignoscendis hominibus* (1492) and *Petris Montis execitiorum, atque artis militaris collectanea in tris libros distincta* (1509).

[104] D. Duarte does not explain what the reasons were.

this book's subject[105]; but, I have done it because I am very fond of wrestling, which I see so undervalued among the important State personalities and others of good lineage that I am very much afraid to see it totally forgotten. Nevertheless, the readers of these lines should remember themselves that this art is one of the most important for the horsemen—and everybody in general—to practice. This is because this art of wrestling gives to those who practice it, many very useful advantages in the art of war, which might be summarized in seven different points[106]:

1. Great improvement in the body fitness (due to the great advantages ensured by the physical work performed when practicing the art of wrestling).

2. Great improvement in the strength of your hands, arms and legs (and in general terms, of your whole body).

3. The feelings of easiness, daringness and confidence, whenever you need to fight another man, using your arms (whatever is your opponent's toughness).

---

[105] Interestingly, while the medieval Italian, German and Spanish sources mentioned previously display a number of mounted wrestling techniques, the closest to linking the two subjects D.Duarte comes in the *Bem Cavalgar* is to say that the subjects are not really linked!

[106] Although probably not his intention here, D.Duarte did indeed discuss the virtues of wrestling once before in his *Regimento pera aprender algunas cousas d'armas* a short essay of advice on how a knight should train at arms. See Hick, Steve, "Dom Duarte and His Advice on Horsemanship," in Stephen Hand, ed., SPADA: An Anthology of Swordsmanship, Chivalry Bookshelf, 2002.

4. Mastery of the techniques of grasping and holding your opponent with your hands and arms, neutralizing his efforts.

5. Knowledge of tricks and cunning use of your feet and body to catch your opponent unready, while using all your strength at the appropriate time; having that knowledge and practice, your body knows what to do at all times.

6. The knowledge and practice of this art of wrestling eliminates all laziness and physical embarrassment you might feel, giving you the incentive to learn other arts because your body is prone to physical activities (and most of the other physical arts are less demanding and dangerous than this one).

7. If you master the art of wrestling you will be praised by lords and their friends, known by strangers and feared by antagonists, due to the advantages everybody knows you have.

Considering all that was written, you will know yourself better, your self-confidence is improved and you are lighted-hearted and self contented for being skilled in the art of wrestling. So, I advise all horsemen — whatever is their knowledge of the art of horse riding — and everybody to whom this might be of interest, to work hard to learn well this art of wrestling and to enjoy its advantages; and those who had the strong will to learn it, will never forget it, while abandoning its practice will bring limitations along with their strength's decrease.

This is the end of Section 5 and the beginning of Section 6

Section 6 - Teaching how to wound using the spurs and their various types; how to control horses[107] using sometimes a wooden stick or a staff

Chapter I - Teaching how to wound using the spurs [108]

The great responsibilities and duties I have to take care of since — in the name of God — I was crowned King, have left me very few moments to dedicate to the writing of this book as I can only do it when it doesn't cause any disturbance to the responsibilities I have.

Respecting the sequence of subjects already established, I am going to address now wounding using the spurs and their various types and how the beasts should sometimes be controlled with wooden sticks or staves; I will briefly give some advice and, mentioning some errors that might be made, I will describe the best ways not to make them and other special warnings that could be useful in some situations.

Wounding with the spurs can be made in a wrong way, by impatience or lack of knowledge, using them in the wrong moments

---

[107] Now that there are no other beasts to be considered (like wild game) the author is back to his initial option, considering *horses* and *beasts* as **synonyms**. I will do the same, in accordance with the author's original words *'cavalos'* and *'bestas'*.

[108] This chapter was written by the author in 1437, after an interruption of 4 years. D. Duarte was crowned King of Portugal in 1433 after the death of his father, King D. João I. Unfortunately D. Duarte died unexpectedly in 1438 and left his book unfinished.

or in an unreasonable manner. There are some who—for lack of knowledge or bad habit—use them when the beast is walking, wounding the beast without any justification or need; if by their nature the beasts are indolent and lazy, the rider should not use the spurs too much because any punishment that is too frequent ceases to get the appropriate results from the beast; if the beast frequently stops abruptly on its forefeet, the solution to correct that is not obtained through the wounding of the beast using the spurs, because it would only increase that imperfection.

If the beast runs well and long distances, there is no worst thing to do than to use the spurs too frequently; for example, a horse which runs well over a league[109] if the rider uses the spurs in a reasonable way, can stop, if it is wounded too much;. due to the incorrect use of the spurs, the beast becomes stale and uncontrollable, and lashes out.

All these errors caused by the too frequent use of the spurs, wounding the beasts too much, are dangerous to the riders due to the beast's reactions and cause difficulties and fatigue and look bad, none of which happen if the riders are skilled. In conclusion, the correct wounding of the beast using the spurs means to use them as needed and at the exact moments needed.

Whenever a rider uses the spurs more than he should, it doesn't look good because the beast doesn't behave with the expected quietness and it is easily understood by many that the rider is not very skilled.

There are also those who make errors through lack of the use of the spurs; it happens mostly to those who are afraid of the beast and also to those who, due to the impatience they feel to wound the beast with the spurs, move the legs so much that are unable to use

---

[109] 5 kms (3.1 miles).

the spurs properly. And these are examples of reasons why the riders do not use the spurs enough.

As far as the use of the spurs at the exact moment is concerned, it is impossible to describe all the situations where wrong decisions about the moment to wound the beast using the spurs were made by the riders; so, I am going to write about some examples of situations where that might happen, with the objective of enabling all riders to identify other situations and consequently to be able to make the appropriate corrections.

1st — In jousts

Some riders wound the horse using the spurs from the starting of the gallop along the *tea* and keep doing it during the run; nevertheless, just before the moment of collision they stop using the spurs to concentrate on the collision; the horse, being afraid of the other jouster and no longer being wounded by the spurs of its rider, either stops abruptly or swerves away. Actually, what the jouster must do is the following[110]:

Not wound the horse with the spurs during its gallop along the *tea* but only just a few moments before the collision, in a reasonable way and in accordance with the beast's nature; if the jouster does it as it should, the beast will not stop its gallop and the collision will happen.

---

[110] The opposite of what was just described.

2nd — Throwing canes or any other things
Much as in the first example, there are those who wound the beasts too much with the spurs at the start of their gallop and have so much attention on the throwing itself that they stop using the spurs and the beast stops; the solution is like the one referred in the first example: the beast should not be wounded with the spurs during the run but only a few moments before the throwing; the spurs should be used with energy and the throwing should be done simultaneously with the beast's increase of its pace.

3rd — When hunting with the spear de soo-braço
Unless you are very much used to wounding with the spurs in those situations, you should not do it while the horse gallops to approach the wild game; but, when you get very close to it, you should use the spurs with energy to ensure that the horse overcomes any fear it might have of the wild game; acting in this way, you avoid your horse stopping before you are in a position to decisively attack the wild game.

4th — When the horse needs to jump over artificial obstacles
Allow the horse to approach the obstacle at a normal gallop's pace and just before the jump, use the spurs with energy just once and stay firm and quiet on the saddle[111] so as not to disturb the horse, to avoiding abruptly stopping instead of jumping.

---

[111] What is described by the author it is a very primitive and incomplete description of everything a show jumping rider actually needs to do, to ensure a correct horse's jump; either it is due to the fact that it is a very brief description (and so, the author was only concerned with the use of the spurs) or the show jumping technique was yet to be born.

5th — To go through people
If the beast usually goes through people without showing signs of resistance, do not use the spurs until you get near; then, use the spurs and the beast will go through people without any problem.

Some additional points:

• You should not energetically wound using the spurs with beasts that are unquiet by nature.

• You should use the spurs appropriately on beasts that are lazy.

• If you need to wound vigorously the beast with the spurs, you should keep your feet firm in the stirrups; those who do not have their feet firm in the stirrups, do not normally know how to wound the beast with the spurs appropriately; so, and besides other advantages, you should keep your feet very firm in the stirrups.

Having in mind all this advice, we can easily understand how important it is to be able to correctly choose the moments and situations to wound the horse using the spurs. So, everyone should know when and how it should be done and — additionally — he should ask for advice from the more knowledgeable ones.

I have no doubts at all that this art — to know how and when to wound the horse using the spurs — is one of the arts essential to the good horsemen; one example of its importance is shown — as a demonstration — by those who, through a very specific use of the spurs, are able to control Sicilian horses in such a way that they move around themselves[112].

---

[112] Like a watch hand fixed in the middle.

There are many errors that can be made in the use of the spurs: incorrect movements of the rider's body and legs, incorrect placement of the feet, wounding the horse too near to the girth (or too far), using the spurs too late or too frequently.   *lead change ?*

To avoid making those errors, you should do the following: do not move your upper body; after you are well mounted on the saddle, do not move the legs above your knees; wound your horse with the spurs with your feet parallel to the horse's belly, neither too near not too far from the girth and always in the same place; as soon you feel your horse's reaction to your use of the spurs, you should withdraw them immediately to avoid to wound the horse too much; do not use the spurs too frequently and pay attention to what the good horsemen do.

What I wrote about the use of the spurs is only valid for our way of riding; I know some Arabs who use very short stirrup straps and so, they keep the heels high up, they wound the beast with their feet in an oblique position relatively to the beast's belly and they use the spurs more frequently than us; and the Irish—who do not use stirrups—do not wound with the spurs as we do.

In conclusion, every country has specific customs that do not cause me any embarrassment because I write mainly to teach my subjects[113] to whom I say that I have written what I believe to be the most advisable.

---

[113] For the first—and only—time in this book, D. Duarte makes a direct reference to his position as King of Portugal, addressing all readers as his subjects

Chapter II — The various types of spurs and how to control the horses using sometimes a wooden stick or a staff

There are spurs of very different types and they are fixed to the rider's feet in various ways.

I have seen them, straight and with a reasonable diameter; curved, either short or long, and bent and pointed toward the bottom; others are bent and pointed toward the top. And some have a shape of a wheel; others have a shape of a tube.

All of them were made having in consideration the specific objectives and habits of their owners. The straight ones and with a reasonable length are mostly used with French saddles and are generally good for all beasts and in every situation; the spurs with a shape of a tube, give some advantages. The spurs in the shape of a wheel are considered according to our custom to be the most beautiful and safe for the beasts, because the wounds they cause are not so big (nevertheless, if the spikes in the rowels are long, the beasts react more to them). The spurs that are bent towards the bottom are more used with horses that get wild, because the rider's legs could stay squeezed to the horse without wounding it too much with the spurs; the long ones are used by riders wearing armor on their legs and by others that do not know to wound using other types. And the spurs that are curved and bent towards the top are mostly appropriate for small beasts who need to be wounded frequently.

Due to ignorance, some riders have spurs that are unsuitable for the horses they are riding. As an example of a totally wrong choice, there are those who wear long and curved spurs, bent towards the top, when their horses are good horses that could get wild.

So, every rider should chose the spurs that are more suitable for the horse he is riding and in accordance with the rider's legs and how he uses them; and if the rider can only afford one type of spurs then, he should chose straight ones of a reasonable length and with small spikes, because they are generally the most appropriate for every situation and beast.

If the rider is using a Gineta saddle, he should have short spurs with small and thick spikes. And all the spurs—independently of their types—should be strong in the iron[114] and should have hinges and straps well fixed to the rider's feet, with the buckle in its proper place, for his advantage and for looking good; if we need to use them unexpectedly and they are weak, the consequence of their use would not be what one might need at the time and I have seen horsemen in great difficulties because of inappropriate spurs. So, they should be good, well made and strong, and their model appropriate to the horseman's legs, to the horse he is riding and to what he plans to use them for.

The rider should not be too concerned with the evolution of local customs because if they are only related to looking good, everyone is entitled to follow or not the changes in local customs, in accordance with his age and his own physical capabilities. But we should always make decisions—to protect ourselves from difficult situations—using the knowledge we have of this art; so, we should not adopt customs that might put ourselves in danger, like for example what I see whenever horsemen are using spurs that are too

---

[114] The author uses the expression *fortes de ferro*; what he means is that all the spurs parts that were made of metal (not necessarily iron) were strong (*fortes*).

Today, the Portuguese use the word *ferro* (**iron** in the English language) in the broad sense of any strong metal and not necessarily iron. As an example of it, in surgery they say the *ferros* to name some of the metal tools or forceps that are used by doctors to help in difficult births.

long. Good horses cannot be well ridden if the rider uses them, and if he is hunting and needs or decides to get out of his horse quickly to go on foot, he might fall down because of the spurs, which will cause mockery among those who are watching and have a good knowledge of this art.

So, the correct decision is to wear spurs of reasonable types — as it was already described — and to reject this bad custom.

We can use wooden sticks and staves to teach and control the beasts in various situations and I am going to give some examples to be considered as advices and warnings to help everybody to find similar ones.

1st — About the teaching of young beasts using the talla[115]

The objective of the use of the *talla* it is not to use the spurs, as they might cause the abrupt stopping of the beast, its movement backwards or running in zigzags; this is because the young beasts — if wounded frequently with the spurs — might start doing some of this malice. And, if we use the talla instead of a wooden stick or a staff, the young beast starts being afraid of the sound of the talla, as well as its lashing; the talla is also used to keep the young beast from getting restless from fear of the bridle, because it is easier to get the young beast used to the talla than to the bridle; so, it is more efficient, because the young beast reacts better to the rider's commands to change direction if he uses the talla, rather than through the use of the bridle.

---

[115] See Glossary.

2nd — After the beasts are used to the harnesses, the simultaneous use of the wounding with the spurs and the strokes with the staff, add the fear of those strokes to the wounding with the spurs. I do not praise this custom very much, even recognizing that it is very commonly used.

Let's assume that a ship is unbalanced because the persons are moving around it and in order to get it right it becomes necessary that everybody stops moving; I say that, if we want to have our beast under control and quiet, we would have a great advantage in using only the wounding with the spurs[116].

Nevertheless, if the beast is used to the simultaneous action of the spurs and the staff, the rider is forced to use both.

3rd — When the beast is malicious and does things such as biting, turning abruptly to the left or rebelling against the rider's control, it is possible to correct it — at least partially — using the staff. God willing, I will speak later on more in detail about it[117].

4th — In times of need — if the bridle or the *barbella*[118] breaks or if the head's harness gets out of its place — the use of the staff (striking the beast's head with it) to force the beast to turn against a wall or to go

---

[116] D. Duarte gave us, throughout his entire book, many comparisons of the highest quality; this is not one of the most successful. Even so, the comparison is there: two disturbance factors to the ship (waves and people) reduced to just one (the waves); two disturbance factors to the beast (spurs and staff) reduced to just one (the spurs).

[117] This subject would have been part of the point 14 referred to in the Introduction of the THIRD PART of this book. Unfortunately, King D. Duarte died before he could finish this project.

[118] See glossary.

to some place where it could not move freely, might help the rider to overcome great dangers. And if the rider doesn't find a suitable place to make the beast stop, there is always the solution of forcing the beast to gallop up a hill to get tired (and easier to be controlled, after having been wounded deep with the spurs).

And having in consideration all I have just said, it is advisable in my opinion, that the horsemen get used to carrying in the hand a wooden stick or a staff, as they might become useful if needed. And, having said this, I end this subject—about the wounding using the spurs, the wooden stick or the staff.

This is the end of Section 6 and the beginning of Section 7

Some teaching about the dangers and disasters that might happen when we are riding and how we can protect ourselves from them— with the help of God.

Section 7[119] - Some teaching about the dangers and disasters that might happen when we are riding and how we can protect ourselves from them — with the help of God

In this Section 7, I am going to write about the reasons why disasters. happen to those who are not good horsemen; and, as they do not know how to take the necessary precautions in advance, I think that the advices I am going to give should be taken in consideration by them.

And they should be aware that any advice given by other person would not be of great value to them unless they are helped and protected by a special grace of our Lord God. And this is in accordance with what it is written:

It is not the one who scatters the seeds and does the irrigation that ensures the harvest, but our Lord God[120].

---

[119] As was mentioned above, D. Duarte died unexpectedly in 1438 and did not finish this book.
Nor did he finish the Part 7; out of the five reasons identified by D. Duarte on the subject of — why we might not know how to protect ourselves from disasters when we are riding — only the first three are addressed by the author.
So, this Part 7 was also left unfinished and it looks to have been written in haste; actually, it looks more like a first draft, rather than a final text.

[120] Paul, First Letter to the Corinthians 3: 7

And I do not think — nor do I for anyone to think — that I presume that my advice to be enough to protect you from all evil things and disasters.

But, in accordance with what it is written:

If you keep only for yourself your reason and knowledge and do not use generosity, you will never reach happiness[121].

So, it appears to me a good personal decision to give this advice, enabling everybody to use it as they think appropriate. And on these subjects — as in everything — we see that — by the grace of God — those who know how to protect themselves from dangers will suffer less.

And I do believe that my advice will be useful, because I have been practicing and learning this science well- namely, the art of being a good horseman; and this is the reason why I have decided to write about it.

In general terms, there are five reasons why we do not know how to protect ourselves from disasters that might happen when we are mounted on a beast:

1. We know so little about this art that we do not know what to do to stay mounted and, falling down, we hurt ourselves.

2. We do not ensure (either ourselves or someone on our behalf) the good quality and the correct placement of all the horse's harness and our own clothes.

3. Our beast is lame or sick, weak, tired, of inconstant nature and acting with malice; so, it is very difficult to control.

---

[121] Ibid., 13:2

4. We do not know how we should protect ourselves in advance of dangers that might occur.

5. We do not know how to neutralize some dangers already in process, from which those who know could save themselves, with the grace of God.

And having said all this, I think that I would be able to give some good advice and teaching to some; those who already know them, would have an opportunity to remember their practice.

About 1: To learn how to avoid falling off the beast, you should reread the THIRD PART—Part 1 of this book (About being STRONG).

You will find there the most important and useful advice about staying strongly mounted on a beast.

About 2: Concerning the beast's preparation and our own, you should also read what was already written about it; nevertheless, having in mind the many situations that might happen, I am going to briefly address those which I think are the most important ones:

About the bridle—You should ensure that all the beast's head straps and reins are strong and that the hinges and the rivets have no defects, avoiding their failure and the consequent accidents. The bridle should be well placed[122](neither high nor low) and the 'barbella' should stay in its appropriate position; this is very

---

[122] This is one of the situations where we should consider that we are dealing with the **bit** and not with the **bridle** itself (see note 2, THIRD PART— Intro.).

important because great accidents might happen if the beast gets unbridled.

About the saddle — It should be of a correct type, according to need; sometimes, accidents happen because the saddles-bows are not well made or the shape of the saddle's flap doesn't have an adequate hollow for the horseman's legs and the saddle's seat might be too long or too short.

About the girth — It should be carefully checked because it must be strong and it needs to be tight around the horse's belly and well placed.

About the stirrups — They should be neither too tight, making it difficult for the horseman to take out his feet, nor too loose, making it impossible for the horseman to keep his feet firm in the stirrups, which is very important to stay strongly mounted. And they should not be too long, because many dangers come from that specific situation — as the experience says; nevertheless, either by caprice or extravagance and not by good custom there are many who use them too long.

About the spurs — They should be of reasonable length ensuring that they cannot get entangled with the horsewhip, either for being too long or for having rowels too big.

About the clothes — They should be neither too tight nor too ample, causing embarrassment to the rider's movements, because they have already been the cause of accidents.

Besides all these there are many similar pieces of advice that might be considered by the readers and that are also related to the beast and to the rider himself.

About 3: There are many different measures related to how we should protect ourselves against beasts who are lame, sick, weak, tired, of inconstant nature or acting with malice; we all should mount and ride those beasts most carefully and in accordance with their flaws, deciding in advance what we should do in every situation that might occur and being very attentive to the correct and appropriate use of our hands, reins and spurs; and I am going to write down some examples, warnings and advice; through them, everybody could think of additional advice to be considered.

If the beasts are lame or weak in the chest, forelegs or forefeet, or if when tired rebel against the bridle, or if they knock the tendons with their shoes,[123] you should be careful to avoid going through hard ground with many rocks, even if there is mud covering them.

---

[123] That's called interfering. The horse will actually be a sloppy mover or lazy, and will catch their own front legs along the back tendon with their other foreleg. We see horses wearing protective boots on their legs to prevent this from happening (and it can happen to both front and back legs).

[216]

The Art of Riding on Every Saddle

If the beasts are carrying loads between the saddle and their heads and if they walk not raising their front feet or forelegs as usual (because eventually they are lame), you should avoid running them through thick woods with plenty of mud, water or high grass.

If the beasts are lame in the gaskins, if they try to get rid of the saddle, if they are sick of the lungs, weak or tired, or if they rear-up, you should be very careful as the beast's weaknesses could cause you great embarrassments.

If the beasts fray their gaskins, if they are skittish or too restless, you should be very careful when going on slopes or through narrow paths.

If the beasts cross their front feet and start running abruptly and crazily, you should be very careful because they are dangerous regardless of the place and situation.

We should always protect ourselves from malicious beasts—wherever we are—as I will later describe, God willing[124]; we should pay special attention to the most dangerous beast's reactions or to those who could put shame on us.

---

[124] A premonition, perhaps?

In the case of the mules, you should avoid going through mud or water, even if it is not too deep.

If the beasts are in season, you should be very careful because they always act maliciously.

If the beasts do not see well and are restless, you should be very careful and avoid riding through places with many trees, caves, piles of rocks, or when is thundering.

You should be very careful if the beasts are running through the woods carrying loads between the saddle and their heads and jump on their front feet; if they rebel against the bridle; if they are weak in the forelegs. You should also avoid riding them through places where the rabbit holes likely are or through soaked barren lands.

DEO GRACIAS[125]

---

[125] This final expression—**Thanks be to God**—is imputed to D.Duarte's copyist.

Glossary

'alymaria' – any wild beast (mainly big game - namely bulls and any other wild beast with horns or antlers, bears and wild boars) hunted by horse riders.

'arondella' – guard firmly fixed to the spear's shaft to protect the rider's hand (with the same objective as the guards of today's swords).

'bandarilhas' – barbed long darts used in bullfights.

'barbella' – curb chain underneath the horse's inferior lip, linked to the bridle (and consequently to the reins).

'[de] Bravante' –riding style and type of saddle commonly used in Portugal (it requires the horseman's legs to stay extended, a little bit forward and the feet firm on the stirrups).

'braçal' – protective armour for the rider's arms.

'cabeçada' – specific headgear of a horse's harness made of the same material as the girth. Additionally protects its face, and also forces the horse to keep its head straight ahead, avoiding it turns it around as it would lose some of its eyesight. If you do not have a 'cabeçada' fitted over the horse's head it is very difficult to fix the bridle.

'gante' – iron glove, gauntlet.

'[de] Gineta' – A riding style and type of saddle that were brought to Portugal by the Arabs from the North of Africa; the horseman's weight is totally supported by the saddle and not by the stirrups.

'gozete' – specific piece fixed to the spear's shaft (made of iron or leather) to ensure a better grasp, avoiding the rider's hand to glide and consequently losing its grip on the correct point of the shaft.

'iluminura' – pictorial ornamentation, adornment of books or manuscripts by designs, an illumination.

'Judeus' - Portuguese word for *Jew*.

'justas' – Jousts

'lança' – Lance / spear

'lança de sobre-mãao' – holding the lance / spear horizontally, resting over the forearm.

'lança de soo-braço' – holding the lance / spear non-horizontally, supported firmly at the armpit.

'lança de soo-mãao' – holding the lance / spear only with the hand.

'marim' – a specific military position among the Arabs of the North of Africa.

'peella' – a game played with a ball and rackets.

'Ruquetes' – The spears used in jousts – the Portuguese way – had the pointed steel head replaced by a round flat surface with three or four embedded small spikes (The *ruquetes*); this way, the physical danger for the jousters was greatly reduced. In late medieval French and English these fixtures were called *rochets*, *rockets* or *coronels* (for the crown-like shape).

'restre' – piece of iron on the breastplate of the rider's armour to support the spear's butt when couched for charging (spear rest). For the maneuvering of light weight spears there is no need of a restre (actually, we could say that the rider's hand is the restre). For the maneuvering of heavy weight spears there is a need of a restre on the rider's breastplate with the rider's hand acting as a second restre, such is the spear's weight.

'sesmaria' – plot of uncultivated land assigned to settlers by the Portuguese Kings (Law signed by King D. Fernando 1367-1383).

talla – horsewhip with only one strip of leather.

'tea' (*teia* in modern Portuguese) – the barrier that separates either the joust field from the spectators or the jousters from each other. A grating (a framework of parallel or crossed wooden or metal bars — from *The Concise Oxford Dictionary*) that separates the jousters between themselves during a joust. They put their horses at gallop starting from the opposite ends and sides of the barrier or tilt.

In all the jousts in Portugal (at least during D. Duarte's years) the riders were separated by a 'tea', running against each other from their opposite ends (and – of course - from the opposite sides of it).

'taris' – type of bridle that is part of the harness commonly used with Gineta saddles.

'travinca' – small piece of wood; making a knot in the reins around that piece of wood we avoid the knot to change position as the piece of wood acts as a brake.

'vara' – lance / spear (as used by D. Duarte in all occasions but one); also a long (1 to 2 meters / 3 to 6 feet) wooden stick (as used by D. Duarte in THIRD PART – Section 6 – Chapter II); this last option is the common meaning of 'vara' in current Portuguese.

Bibliography

Editions:

• Piel Joseph M., ed. *'Livro da ensinança de bem cavalgar toda sela'* *que fez Elrey Dom Eduarte de Portugal e do Algarve e Senhor de Ceuta -* *Ed. crítica, acompanhada de notas e dum glossário.* Lisbon: INCM (Imprensa Nacional – Casa da Moeda) 1944.

• *'Livro da ensinança de bem cavalgar toda sela', escrito pelo Senhor* *Dom Duarte, Rei de Portugal e do Algarve e Senhor de Ceuta, transcrito* *do manuscrito extante na Biblioteca Real de Paris.* Lisbon: Typ. Rollandiana, 1843.

• *'Leal Conselheiro', escrito pelo Senhor Dom Duarte, Rei de Portugal e* *do Algarve e Senhor de Ceuta, transcrito do manuscrito extante na* *Biblioteca Real de Paris.* Lisbon: Typ. Rollandiana, 1843.

Other Works:

• Pereira, Carlos Henriques. *Étude du premier traité d'équitation* *portugais.* Paris: L'Harmattan, 2001.

• Peres, Damião and Eleutério Cerdeira. *Edição Monumental da* *História de Portugal.* Barcelos: Portucalense Editora, 1928

• Pina, Ruy de. *Crónicas do Rei D. Duarte.* Edited by M. Lopes de Almeida. Tesouros da Literatura e da História. Porto : Lello & Irmão, 1977

Preto, Jorge. *Pretos de Portugal e do Brazil.* Editora - Mensageiro da Fé, Ldª. Salvador-Bahia, Brasil, 1976.

• Saraiva, José Hermano. *História Concisa de Portugal*, 3rd ed. Colecção SABER, Publicações Europa-America no. 123. Mem Martins: Francisco Lyon de Castro, 1978

• Serrão, Joaquim Veríssimo. *História de Portugal,* 3rd edition. Póvoa do Varzim, Viseu and Cacém: Editorial VERBO, 1977.

• Sousa, Manuel de. *Reis e Rainhas de Portugal,* 6th ed. Mem Martins: SPORPRESS, 2000.

An Amateur Historian's research and interpretation of History

Can we describe some of the characteristics of an amateur Historian?

He is (usually) a very sceptical type of researcher.

He doesn't believe in a 'story' - even if it is written the same way by many - if there are no real facts supporting it or if he finds (even small) discrepancies.

He loves to research to the deepest level of detail, he goes after as many possible sources as he can find and - <u>because it's a hobby for him</u> - he has 'all the patience in the world' to do it.

He just loves to be able to stand up against the so called 'established truth' - as it was/is written by professional Historians – being able to raise some doubts, which lead a totally different 'version of the truth'.

In summary, he is a troublemaker and - frequently - an annoying person for not accepting lightly the 'established truth'!

So, he is the antithesis of a professional Historian , who - in many situations - conforms himself to circumstances and says **<u>'let it be'</u>** (not having the time to look in depth for the reasons behind any discrepancies he finds).

Let me illustrate it with an example.

There are hundreds (literally) of these images spread all over Portugal (and in 'thousands' of books). The same very serious face and always wearing the same type of hat (a large brim hat as used in Burgundy in the first half of the XV century).

There is even a XX century marvellous monument by the seaside in Lisbon acknowleging and honoring the Portuguese discoveries, in which the first sculpture (leading the way) shows the same 'person':

<u>Everybody</u> knows who is he!

Prince D. *Henrique,* widely known as 'prince **Henry, the Navigator'** (brother of King D. *Duarte* of Portugal), of course!.

Right?

The professional Historian says: Yes, or at least, <u>'Let it be'</u>!

The annoying amateur Historian goes further and says:

The then Prince D. *Duarte* negotiated for two long years (1428-1429) directly with emissaries of *Filipe* III, Duke of Burgundy and Count of Flanders, in the matter of his marriage to D. *Duarte's* only sister *Isabel,* Princess of Portugal. The wedding took place in Bruges (at the time it was one of the most important trading towns in Europe) on 7 January 1430.

D. *Duarte* - crowned as King of Portugal in 1431 - was well known in Burgundy (considered as the cultural centre of Europe in the first half of the XV century) and that one of the most important Burgundy painters produced in the early 1430's a most amazing paint of '*Le Roy du Portyall*' (King D. *Duarte*):

Additionally there isn't even one single portrait of either D. *Duarte* or his brother D. *Henrique* (it is a fact!).

Nevertheless 'everybody' is saying that the guy wearing the burgundy hat is Prince D. *Henrique* (who never had any connection with Burgundy) and not D. *Duarte* himself. Sounds, at the very least, strange! Which leads us to some further research.?

About King D. *Duarte* of Portugal and his brother prince D. *Henrique*

Mr. *António Belard da Fonseca* was a Portuguese professional historian who, as many others, spent some time (during the second half of the XX century) in the interpretation of the most famous Portuguese painting from the XV century.

He also produced the following statement:

Os erros e as mentiras, históricas ou artísticas, tal como as pessoas, merecem toda a veneração e deferência quando atingem determinada idade.

«The errors and the lies, historic or artistic, as the individuals, deserve all the veneration and deference when they attain a certain age».

I am going to describe for you what I (as many others much more 'illustrious' than me) consider to be the most important Portuguese example of an historic lie and which, as you've probably gathered by now, is about the picture of Prince D. *Henrique*.

[229]

'Everybody' knows him, right?
(Always shown with the same type on large hat on his head).

Question – Is it the real picture of Prince 'D. *Henrique*'? It looks like, but...

.... I say that - in my opinion - it is not!

It is - most probably - of King D. *Duarte*!

To explain/prove this statement let me present to you the most famous example of the XV century Portuguese painting.

The Six Panels of 'S. *Vicente de Fora*'

**(This marvellous masterpiece can be seen at the
Museu de Arte Antiga in Lisbon)**

This painting measures:

2.07 meters high by .64 - .60 – 1.28 – 1.28 - .60 - .64 meters wide
(left to right).

It is oil painted on wood and its author is considered (by most) to have been *Nuno Gonçalves* (a painter of the court of King D. *Afonso V*, son of King D. *Duarte*) who painted it around 1450.

The Lisbon earthquake of 1755 (estimated to have reached 9 in the Richter scale) destroyed most of the city and the paintings were only (re)discovered in 1882 in the monastery of <u>S. Vicente de Fora</u>. This is the reason why this masterpiece is known as '<u>The six panels of S. Vicente de Fora</u>'.

All the documentation about it disappeared and many historians and painting specialists spent 'years' to produce a reasonable and logic interpretation about it (namely identifying the various personalities). Hundreds of articles, pages (many of them in the internet) and several books were produced about it.

I've studied in detail the two most comprehensive ones: one in the internet (putting together the opinions of several specialists) and a 200-page book produced in 1994 (its title is 'The Keys of the Mystery', which I consider to show a bit of immodesty from the author).

The fact is that <u>both interpretations</u> state (prove in some way) that Prince D. *Henrique* is not represented in the 3rd panel from the left.

The first interpretation says (through a quite logical justification) that the picture in the 3rd panel from the left, wearing a large brown hat, is in fact of <u>King D. Duarte</u> (already dead at the time the painting was produced).

It also affirms that Prince D. *Henrique* is the kneeled nobleman shown in the 5th panel from the left and 'proves' it comparing his head and face against the sculpture on his tomb (and we have to accept that the similarities are too evident to be ignored).

Now going back to the 3rd panel from the left, known by many as **'The Kings' Panel'**, (**'o painel dos REIS'**, in the Portuguese language), allows me to present a very strong interpretation that concludes that the serious man praying, dressed in dark and wearing a large rim burgundy hat is **King D. Duarte**, already dead at the time of the painting.

Here is an enlarged view of the 3rd panel from the left:

The chosen interpretation basically says the following:

There is a family around the 'Saint' .

Grand-Father (**AVÔ** in the Portuguese language) - *Duarte*, praying.

Grand-Mother (**AVÓ** in the Portuguese language) - *Leonor*, with a rosary/chaplet (a string of beads for counting prayers) over her vest.

Being already dead at the time the painting was produced, they are both 'poorly' dressed in sombre colours and wearing no jewellery or adornments (as if they were from 'another world'). There is a great contrast between them and the other four main personalities in the panel.

Father (**PAI** in the Portuguese language) - King *Afonso V*, kneeling

Mother (**MÃE** in the Portuguese language) - Queen *Isabel*, also kneeling

Son (**Filho** in the Portuguese language) - 10-12 years old boy *João* (future King D. *Afonso V*)

It is indeed quite a strong interpretation!

Making it appropriate to recollect Mr. *António Belard da Fonseca's* statement:

«The errors and the lies, historic or artistic, as the individuals, deserve all the veneration and deference when they attain a certain age».

'Should we fight against the tide'?(Let it be...) says the professional Historian.

However, being merely an amateur Historian, I'll take the liberty of sharing another mystery (<u>or another historic lie</u>):

It is about the tomb of King D. *Duarte* and his wife, Queen Dª. *Leono,r* located in the *Batalha* monastery (their sculptures on top of the tomb show them side by side and hand-in-hand).

There is a major discrepancy in what it is written there, and one which is impossible for me to present a reasonable explanation for, but still worth analysing.

Please, keep in mind that our King's first name in the XIX-XV centuries was *Eduarte* and that this first name disappeared from the

Portuguese language being replaced by two options: *Duarte* or *Eduardo*.

<u>What is written in the tomb? (in the Latin language)</u>

EDUARD I PORTUGAL & ALGARVE REX & REGINA ELEONORA UXOR ...

(Eduardo I, Rei de Portugal e do Algarve e sua Esposa a Rainha Leonor...) - in the Portuguese language

(Edward I, King of Portugal and Algarve and his wife the Queen Leonor...) - in the English language.

How is it possible? If History decided that our King *Eduarte* was to be known as *Duarte* how could we get an explanation for the name <u>EDUARD</u> in the tomb?

Only if (in the Latin language) the name *Eduarte* was to be written as Eduard!

<u>Is this another mystery/historic lie or 'just' a mistake</u>?!

From my research I got 7 Latin forenames that were converted to Edward in English and to *Eduardo* in Portuguese (but none of them as *Eduarte* or *Duarte,* who never existed in the Latin language) ...

Edonardus

Edrus

Eduardum

Eduardus

Edwardi

Edwardum

Edwardus

...and the forename **Eduard** (as it is engraved in the tomb) **never existed,** neither in Latin nor in the Portuguese language!

In the end, the troublemaker amateur Historian is pleased (even if he got nowhere...).

The mystery stays.

Perhaps the specialist who engraved on the tomb stone didn't know the Latin language or just made a mistake and engraved a non-existent forename (quite trivial explanations, aren't they? ...).

But that error doesn't explain why our King *Eduarte* is historically known as *Duarte* and not as *Eduardo*.

The 'troublemaker' is pleased once again. He established a total confusion around a detail[126] that 'nobody' approached ever before. 'Everybody' was - and is - pleased with the 'established truth'! Duarte? Let it be, say the professional Historians...

And there is no explanation in sight...but nobody cares... there is one 'established truth' accepted by most...that's what matters!

Let it be , **'they all' say!**

Long life to the amateur Historians!

António Franco Preto   **March 2011**

---

[126] Is it important the real forename of a King? The amateur Historian thinks it is...

[239]

Printed in Great Britain
by Amazon.co.uk, Ltd.,
Marston Gate.